Teens in Transition

A Guide for Teens: Finishing High School and Making It in College

Teens in Transition

by

Jack D. Bachman

For additional copies, please contact:

Answer Publications

P.O. Box 550 - Roanoke, Indiana 46783
(260) 478-5500
www.answerpublications.com

First Edition, 2005
Second Printing

International Standard Book Number:
0-9763919-2-9

All Scripture quotations are from the King James Bible.

Printed and bound in the United States of America
Faith Baptist Church Publications
Ft. Pierce, Florida
www.fbcpublications.com

Dedication

There are many to whom I owe a great deal of thanks and honor. Those who have invested in me, contributed to my life, believed in me, and loved me. In choosing someone to whom I would dedicate this book, many names crossed my mind and heart. Though all of them were worthy and important, I could not help but admit that one seemed to stand out above the rest. I would like to dedicate this book to my wife, Robyn.

She not only has been a great wife and a wonderful mother, but she also has been my partner in the ministry. She has attended nearly every youth activity, teen camp, youth conference, missions trip, banquet, and special meeting to which I have taken our teenagers or which I have conducted myself. She has swallowed goldfish, taken pies to the face, participated in skits, dressed up like an old bag lady, and done some things at which even I am astounded -- just because she loves me and she loves our teenagers. She has fixed hundreds of meals and thousands of plates of food for our teens, feeding them nearly every week for teen soulwinning and doing most of the cooking and food planning for yearly banquets and retreats. She has taught our teen girls in Sunday school and has been a friend, a counselor, and a "second mom" to many of them through the years. She has been my eyes, my ears, and my sixth sense to pick up on the things I often overlook or am too involved to notice. She has prayed for our teens, laughed with our teens, wept for our teens, and lived for our teens. She has allowed me to share my heart with them and in her own heart adopted them as our own. I know of no other youth pastor's wife in America more involved with her husband's ministry than my wife has been.

There are many who have helped to mold me and fashion me over these past 35 years, but no one is doing more to continue to help me day by day than my wife. As is said of the virtuous woman in Proverbs 31, my heart doth safely trust in her so that I will have no need of spoil. God knew I would need a great deal of help along the way, and He prepared and fashioned a lady who would meet my needs. What a blessing to have a wife that is a help, meet (fit) for me. I love you, Robyn!

Acknowledgments

I want to express my appreciation first of all to my father, Pastor James Bachman, for encouraging me to write this book as well as for his great example to me through the years. The majority of the contents of these pages are a result of my parents teaching and training me in the way that I should go. I am honored to be their son and thankful to God for allowing me to have the heritage that I do.

I also am grateful to my youth pastor, Ricky Moon, as well as another great influence on my life, Dr. Jeff Owens. These two men played a huge role in my years as a "teen in transition." Though I could write a whole chapter of thanks to the numerous people who have invested in me, these two deserve a special recognition for that era of my life.

I also would like to say a word of thanks to Vicky Pope for her hours of proofreading and to my brother, Mark, for inspiring me to write a couple important missing chapters as well as for his vote of confidence.

My appreciation is also expressed to Kelly Finton, Chantha Chhim, and Jonathan Wells for their assistance and ideas on a cover design.

Teens in Transition

Foreword

What is "senioritis?" How can you avoid it? This book is <u>full</u> of sound advice, especially for people who are in their late teens! Bro. Bachman knows what he is talking about. He has been through this exciting; but dangerous period. Read it and heed it. Read the advice of Dr. Jack Hyles about this perplexing time in your life. Read how Bro. Bachman had a wonderful, moral plan for his life. It was <u>all</u> planned in detail but he left God out of his plans! Is that what <u>you</u> are doing?

I have been on the administration of Hyles-Anderson College ever since its inception 33 years ago. Bro. Jack Bachman is one of the finest young men we have ever graduated. <u>Read his book</u>!

Dr. Wendell Evans

*President
Hyles-Anderson College*

Introduction

I cannot overemphasize to you the importance of this book. This is true not because of the author, not because of the subject, not even because of the content, but rather because of the consequences of not following the advice you are about to read. I know of few periods of your life more important, more vital, and more vulnerable than your senior year of high school through your first few years of college. I have seen the devil ruin more lives, wreck more testimonies, and waste more potential in this stage of life than in any other.

So much transition is taking place in your life as you move from high school days into college life. You are changing physically, emotionally, mentally, spiritually, and socially. There is a huge transition taking place in your finances, your responsibilities, your relationships, your maturity, your interests, your focus, your goals, your career, and your views. You are beginning to fend for yourself, think for yourself, pay for yourself, decide for yourself, and believe in yourself. You are finding out how much you know and how much you have yet to learn. You are realizing how busy you are and how easy you had it when you thought you were busy before. You are seeing how independent you are and how much you miss Mom's cooking and Dad fixing your car. You are becoming aware of how expensive life can be and how much work it takes to make ends meet. You are learning what it means to have multiple "irons in the fire" and are learning to cope with balancing them all. These are exciting days, but apprehensive days. These are victorious days, but tiring days. These are learning days, but confusing days. These are fun days, but busy days. These are maturing days, but expensive days. These are dating days, but lonely days. These are informative days, but days full of questions. These are days to which you have looked forward, but days to which you will spend much time looking back. These are days you can never relive, but days that may be some of the best of your life. These are days that are potentially successful, but days that are just as potentially dangerous.

Read carefully and ask God to help you protect your future by the things you learn. Much is riding on what you do during these vital years of your life. Bathe them in prayer, seek godly counsel, stay in God's Word, and don't get in too big of a hurry concerning some of the biggest decisions of your life that you will be making over the next few months and years. I hope this book will help guide you through one of the most exciting, and yet most vulnerable, times of your life.

Chapter 1

Protecting Your Potential

The forming of your character begins very early in life. More than likely your parents did not wait until you were a teenager to teach you a good work ethic, responsibility, honesty, cleanliness, kindness, and purity. From the time you were old enough to crawl and touch things that were breakable, you started to hear the word "no" and feel the stinging hand that went along with disobedience. (It is no wonder one of the first words kids learn to say is "no" and one of the first actions they learn is shaking their head back and forth!) Ever since those days, your parents have poured their time, their money, their sweat, their tears, their love, and their dreams into you. Along the way you have also probably had a teacher, a coach, a grandparent, a Sunday school teacher, a relative, a pastor, and/or a youth director investing much to get you to the point you are today. All this effort, all this training, all this molding and fashioning was for a purpose -- that you might make something of your life, reach your potential, and please the Lord. You have no idea the long hours, the hard-earned dollars, the sleepless nights, and the tearful prayers that have been a part of your life thus far. In many ways, the investment of all these people is now being placed in your hands. What you do in the next few years may make your life one of success and rejoicing or make it one of ruin and heartache.

The Bible says in **III John 4, "I have no greater joy than to hear that my children walk in truth."** As a parent, I know that this is true of my feelings toward my own children. There is nothing any more rewarding and thrilling than to see my children pleasing God and doing right. I also know that as John wrote this Epistle, he was speaking of people beyond the realms of his own biological children. Being a youth pastor, a coach, a Christian school teacher, a Sunday school teacher, and a bus captain, I know this also is true regarding other "children" in whose lives God has allowed me to be a part. The dream and goal of your Christian parents, teachers, and pastor is that you will be happy and successful -- not in the eyes of the world but in the eyes of God. So much potential lies in your power, and what you do with it will determine not only their happiness but yours.

The flesh, the world, and the devil will be working overtime to influence these next vital years of your life and the important choices you will be making during them. In the next several months, you will be making some life-altering, life-forming, lifetime decisions -- where you will go to college, what career you will study and pursue, and whom you might marry. I beg of you, protect your potential. Much has been invested in you to get you to this point. Don't throw it all away with a rash decision, a night *of pleasure, an experiment with sin, or following the wrong people.*

For years as a youth pastor I have watched young people reach their senior year of high school and their first summer after graduation and throw away in a few months, a few weeks, or even a few moments a potential that many people who love them have spent years trying to build. I have watched teens who were active, faithful, respectful, soulwinning, Bible-reading, separated young people, quit church, quit serving, quit soulwinning, quit dressing right, quit walking with God, quit being moral, and quit pursuing the joyful life they could have had.

What makes this part of your life so vulnerable? I believe it can be many things, but let us look at three of the most common.

1. Freedom

All of a sudden you begin to get privileges you didn't have before. You can drive yourself anywhere you want. You don't have to be tied to school schedules or school rules. You are out of the youth group and out from under its guidelines. Your parents may give you more slack and extend your curfew. There is nothing wrong with freedom, but you must know that with freedom comes responsibility. You may find yourself being pushed into an era of freedom that you do not yet have the character or experience to

17

handle. Don't swallow the misconception that getting a diploma means you have the right to do what you want, when you want, where you want, how you want, and with whom you want. In chasing this new-found freedom, you would likely run right into sin and out of God's will. A marriage that could have been blessed, a ministry that could have been successful, a testimony that could have been clean, and a life that could have been happy never will be if you get ruined by freedom. Don't allow freedom to rob you from your potential.

2. Money

At this stage in your life you are getting employment, and with that job comes a paycheck. With that money comes a desire to buy things that you previously could not afford. I would like to point out that just as there is nothing wrong with freedom, there is nothing wrong with money. Unfortunately, if you don't have the character to control your money or control the appetites it feeds, you are going to end up in trouble. The Bible puts it this way in **I Timothy 6:10, "For the love of money is the root of all evil: which while some coveted after, they erred from the faith, and pierced themselves through with many sorrows."** Oh, how many teenagers I have seen quit church, quit soulwinning, quit working a bus route, and quit coming to activities just to work a few more hours. It was not that they needed the money to survive, but to buy the things they wanted to have or *to start saving for college because they had already blown their first three months of paychecks on clothes, cars, video games, and foolishness. How many times too have I seen them get a job and the taste for money and then never go to Bible college like they planned because they have a "good" job they don't want to give up. That job then keeps them out of church, out of service, and out of the place of the will of God where they may have found their future mate. Don't allow the love of money to rob you of your potential.*

3. The lack of personal standards and convictions

You see, for years you have grown up obeying mom and dad's rules, the preacher's convictions, the youth pastor's policies, and the school's handbook. All of a sudden, when thrust out on your own, you may realize you don't know what you believe or why you believe it. The flesh starts calling loudly, the world starts pulling strongly, and the devil starts whispering softly and it is easy to decide to do that which is right in your own eyes. In reality, you may have no personal standards or Bible convictions. You might simply have done what you were made to do and never even taken the time to find out what God's Word said. You went soulwinning because there was a teen soulwinning program and your friends went. You dressed modestly because there were school rules dictating what you could and couldn't wear. You went to church faithfully because your parents took you. You listened to the right music because that was the only music in the house. Now that you are on your own, it becomes evident what you really believe. All too often the answer is "nothing." You had better work hard at finding out what the Bible says about what you should do, what you shouldn't do, and how you should live and why. Don't just have Mama's standards or when Mama is gone, you won't do right. Don't just have the preacher's convictions or when the preacher is gone, you won't follow them. Get in your Bible and find out where they got those beliefs and make them your own. Don't decide to chuck everybody's beliefs and come up with your own standard of living. Ask them to help you see in God's Word what His standard of living is and then make it yours! Don't allow your lack of personal convictions to rob you of your potential.

I trust that many years from now your parents, your teachers, your coaches, your pastor, and your youth director will be able to look at your life and have "no greater joy," seeing you still walking in the truth. I also hope that you will be able to look at yourself in the mirror or look down into the eyes of one that calls you "Mommy" or "Daddy" and thrill to know that the labor of many was not in vain -- you worked hard to protect your potential!

Chapter 2

Protecting Your Memories

You had better sit down if you are not already. I have some very bad news. You are at an extremely high risk to catch a disease that is nearly unavoidable. Though the disease is temporary, it can cause symptoms and consequences from which you will never recover. People your age are contracting it by the hundreds of thousands and usually without even realizing it. It is called "senioritis" -- that's right, a destructive thing caught during your senior year of high school. It may begin as early as September, often by the end of Christmas break, and almost definitely by spring break. Read closely the list of symptoms to see if you may have contracted a case of senioritis.

1.   *Anxiousness to hurry and be done with school*
2.   *Working all the hours you can to save as much money as possible*
3.   *Lack of ability to concentrate for your spelling test*
4.   *Large stacks of college brochures and catalogs in your room*
5.   *Limited desire to be with under-classmen, especially junior-highers*
6.   *Nightmares about getting lost on your way to your first college class*
7.   *Making a sign-up list to pass around for all those*

wanting to date you

8. *Making a list of which ten people you want to date (the first week!)*
9. *Skipping youth activities to pick out college luggage*
10. *Skipping teen soulwinning to start packing that luggage (for next year!)*
11. *Planning during high school chapel which college major to take*
12. *Thinking juniors are so immature*
13. *Making a list for your parents of all the things they should buy you*
14. *Buying new college outfits every week*
15. *Not asking for counsel on where to go to college because you already made up your mind*
16. *Not listening to counsel because you know what you are doing*
17. *Skipping teen camp because you are just too busy this year*
18. *Hanging out with college-agers or young adults instead of teenagers*
19. *Wishing your parents would stay off your case and give you a break*
20. *Thinking you don't have senioritis*

If you are experiencing any one or more of these symptoms, please seek help immediately.

You see, senioritis comes because you are now so close to graduating and going to college that those become the only things on which you can focus. Now don't get me wrong; there is nothing wrong with planning, thinking ahead, setting goals, and preparing. The problem is that you will become so enamored with and consumed by the future that you will miss out on the present. This is the last chance you will have to be in high school, to be in the youth department, to go to youth activities, to go on teen soulwinning, to play high school sports, to affect your permanent high school grades, to go to teen camp or youth conferences, to live at your parents' house as a "non-adult," to go to the Sunday School teen department, and to make high school memories. Don't cheat yourself out of an exciting part of your present because you have gotten too wrapped up in your future. Yes, you need to plan, to prepare, to work, to save, and even to dream for your college years; but don't miss out on the opportunities and memories of your last chance to be a teenager!

1. Get the best grades possible your senior year.

Your GPA is a part of your permanent record that will follow you the rest of your life. Potential employers will look at it, the college you attend will look at it, your car insurance company may look it, and one day your kids might even look at it. End your high school career on a good note and study hard, work hard, do any extra credit available, and get the best grades you can.

2. Don't miss out on any teen activity, teen camp, conferences, or trips.

You don't understand the memories you are making

as a teenager. I promise you, there will be many days that you will want to go back to the youth department. The first summer you come home from college, you will be wishing you could go to the youth activities and on teen outings. You will walk by the teen department on Sunday morning and want to go into that class. Then it will be too late. Now is your opportunity to make as many memories as possible. Don't miss a thing. You will probably be working to earn money for college, as well you should. Make sure your employer knows up front when he hires you the days you will need off for teen functions. This is your last chance to be a part of the youth group. Protect your memories and don't let senioritis rob them from you.

3. Stay active in church and as involved as possible in service.

I have seen many young people get a job so they can start saving money for Bible college and then allow their job to keep them out of Wednesday night church, out of teen soulwinning, out of working a bus route, out of Sunday school, out of a walk with God, and all too often out of God's will. You will have the rest of your life to be working a job. Don't get so consumed with it that you allow it to keep you from staying active and faithful in church. You are preparing to go off to Bible college. Don't get so spiritually weak that when it's time to go, you just decide not to go at all. You don't have to work a job *that would knock you out of church in order to earn enough money to go to college. You need to work a job where you can stay active in church and better manage the money you make.*

Don't just be in church for every service, but listen closely to every message. You are entering a phase of your life in which you will be making very important decisions, and you need to listen intently to all the biblical counsel and preaching you can get. Head off to Bible college at a spiritual strong point in your life, not in the midst of a spiritual famine.

4. Don't become exclusive with the senior class.

Now granted, there is a natural camaraderie with those graduating from high school together, as well there should be. But for some reason, when senioritis hits, all other teenagers seem to become immature, scum-of-the- earth, second-class citizens. Many of these people are teens with whom you have spent the last several years and whom you have considered your close friends. Some you may have even grown up with through grade school. Don't throw away all those years of friendship just because they are not a "big, cool, mature senior" like you. As is the case with many symptoms of senioritis, those who have it often don't even realize what is happening. I have spent much time counseling with juniors and sophomores who were wondering what they did, that all of a sudden their good friend or even best friend (the senior with senioritis) no longer wants to spend much time with them. Again, this is your only chance to build memories with this group of people. You will have several years to build relationships with college kids and adults. Don't jump to the next phase of your life yet. Protect your memories with your younger peers.

5. Don't pull away from your parents.

Another common symptom of senioritis is when a senior starts getting super independent and weakening the relationship with his mom and dad. Now I understand, you are maturing, you are growing up, you are becoming your own man (or woman), and you are learning to fend for yourself. No problem, but don't let this independence drive you away from showing your love, respect, appreciation, and honor to your parents. Be careful to watch your tongue and make sure you are still very respectful. A diploma doesn't authorize you to stop saying "Yes, ma'am" and "Yes, sir" to your mom and dad. Being a senior doesn't make it right for you to start "telling" your parents things instead of "asking" them. Instead of saying, "Hey, mom, I'm going over to so-and-so's house," try asking, "Mom, would it be all right with you if I went over to so-and-so's house?" See the difference? Don't think that you are too big and tough, Mr. Senior, to tell your mom and dad "I love you." Don't get into a mode where you think they owe you a big, fancy open house, or a car, or anything. Show appreciation for everything they give you. If you are so big and independent, then how about you offering to pay for your open house and all the food? Maybe you can pay for the car to get you to work, the insurance to put the car on the road, the tires you burn up every time you drive, the food to put on the table, the house payment so you have a place to put your head, the house insurance, the health insurance, the life insurance, the heat bill, the water bill, the electric bill, and the phone bill. Maybe you can even reimburse them the over $100,000 it has taken to raise you. Didn't think so! Remember all they have done for you and invested in you before you back talk or get a little too big for your britches. Realize you are privileged to live in their home and they deserve to be treated with honor no matter how old you are or how independent you think you have become. I beg you, use these last few months in their home to build memories that you will not regret and that you will cherish for years to come. This is your last chance to influence what your parents remember of you as their teenage son or daughter. Don't blow it if you already have a good relationship, and improve it if you don't. As one music teacher taught me years ago, if you start on a good note and end on a good note, sometimes people will overlook what they heard in the middle. Make your last few notes pleasant in your parents' ears. Protect your memories with your mom and dad.

Let me conclude this chapter with an analogy I heard

Dr. Jack Hyles often give. Your life is much like doing a load of laundry in a washing machine. Each stage of your life -- infant years, childhood, junior age, junior high, senior high, college, marriage, parenting, middle age, senior, and elderly years -- is like one of those cycles. If you skip certain cycles or rush certain cycles, your life will not end up as you intended or as it could have. Live every cycle to its fullest. Enjoy this cycle and don't rush to the next cycle until this one is complete. You can never go back to these teen years. Make all the memories you can make. End on a high note. Move to your next cycle without regret. This is your last chance, senior. Don't fall victim to senioritis. Decide you will protect your memories.

Chapter 3

Protecting Your College Decision

Very few decisions in your life will be as important as the decision as to if and where you go to college. This decision will more than likely also greatly influence whom you will marry. It will be a large part of your character molding and preparation for life. It will affect the degree to which you will be a success in your field of study and future career. It will determine where you will be taught much, learn much, and grow much. If chosen unwisely, it may be where you ruin your future potential, your future marriage, your future ministry, and your future testimony. Other than your decision about salvation and your decision on whom to marry, this may very well be the most important decision of your entire life. With so much riding on this choice, I think it would be very wise to establish some principles to help guide you along the way. Again, make your decision based on these qualifications. Hold your potential college choices up to these principles and choose the one God shows you aligns the best.

1. Seek, listen to, and follow godly counsel from godly counselors.

I cannot overemphasize the importance of this point. God has given you some people in your life to help direct you and guide you when you are sailing through uncharted waters. First of all, your parents, your pastor, your youth pastor, and other godly counselors have not only likely been through this process themselves but have also probably helped others with these same decisions. They have been around long enough to see the results and fruit of those who have chosen a good path and those who have not. They have a very important advantage called "experience" that you do not have. You would be very wise to tap into that valuable resource. Where your buddies and friends want to go to college or think you should go to college is not a good guiding principle because they have no more experience than you do. Not only do these counselors have wisdom that comes through experience, but they also have wisdom that comes through responsibility. You see, these people have to give an account to God one day on your behalf. In Hebrews 13:17 God says, "Obey them that have the rule over you, and submit yourselves: for they watch for your souls, as they that must give account, that they may do it with joy, and not with grief: for that is unprofitable for you." Authorities who realize this are going to walk close to the Lord and ask for His direction for your life. They love you and want what is best for you. It would serve you well to ask for their advice, listen to their advice, and follow their advice.

My wife's father got saved later in life while serving in the Air Force. Shortly after that, he picked up a <u>Sword of the Lord</u> *newspaper and read about a man named Jack Hyles. He was amazed. He read more and more and even heard some of his preaching tapes. The more he heard this man preach, the more he liked what he was hearing. When my wife graduated from high school, she started trying to decide where she should go to college. Her dad told her, "Robyn, I believe God wants you to go to Hyles-Anderson." She didn't want to go to Hyles-Anderson, but she loved her daddy and honored his wishes. If you ask her now about that decision, she would undoubtedly tell you it was one of the best decisions of her life. Even though her dad knew very little of this place in Hammond, because he was her daddy, God gave him insight as to what was best for his daughter. There are so many times that God will lay on the heart of a pastor, a parent, or some other godly counselor His will for your life, but you miss it because you don't ask, you ask but don't follow, or you ask but don't even hear because you have already made up your mind. The Bible says in* **Proverbs 11:14, "Where no counsel is, the people fall: but in the multitude of counselors there is safety."** *So your choices are simple -- fall or find safety. Listen to your God-given counselors!*

2. Seek God's will above your own or anyone else's.

The words, "I want to go to..." or "I think I should go

to..." should never preface your answer concerning where you will attend college. So many young people mess up this important decision basing it on what they want or what some friend wants. God says in **Matthew 6:33, "But seek ye first the kingdom of God, and his righteousness; and all these things shall be added unto you."** Don't throw God's will in as just another factor in your decision. Make it the only factor in your decision. It is what is really important. Bear with me while I give a word of testimony.

As a young boy I remember playing cops and robbers with my brother. Oh, the thrill of this game! We would chase each other around the house or around the yard for hours on end. I was always "Unit 12" and would respond to the call on my make-believe walkie-talkie, get into my make-believe squad car, turn on my make-believe siren, arrive on the make-believe crime scene, pull my make-believe gun, and struggle to catch and arrest this violent, criminal brother of mine. I knew right from those days of cops and robbers that I wanted to be a policeman when I grew up. There were only a few problems. I was saved, my daddy was a preacher, I went to church, and I heard preaching on "the will of God." Now granted, I am sure for some people it is God's will for them to be in law enforcement. In my case though, I never bothered asking God about it just in case He would spoil my plans by saying something else. As I grew older, I began to correspond with and even got to know a few police officers. On my own, I went to the library and got books on criminal investigation and law enforcement. At a youth conference in Hammond, Indiana one year, God began dealing with my heart. I realized I was being a little selfish with my life and needed to find some way to serve God. I developed a plan. I decided I would go to Pensacola, Florida, and study law enforcement. After graduating from there, I then would go to the Michigan State Police Academy and take my required police training. I would become a police officer at the State Police post in Muskegon, Michigan, and live in Spring Lake, Michigan. I made plans for my house. I chose a plot of land on which to build that house. I talked to the owner of the land who agreed to sell me that plot and help me build my house. I would then remain a state policeman until I turned 35 years of age, just to give me experience. The year I turned 35, the State Police chaplain of Michigan was going to retire. I would take his place. (I was told at that time, in the mid 1980's, he was making around $100,000 a year.) As the new state chaplain, I would begin going from post to post across the state, finding nearby fundamental, Baptist churches and asking them to supply a volunteer chaplain for their nearby post. I would also help him establish weekly services to be held at the post as well as provide godly counsel and support for the officers as needed. Once I had established this situation in every State Police post in Michigan, I would then begin going state by state, leading each state chaplain to the Lord and helping him establish the same system in his own state's *posts. What a master-mind plan I had developed. I would get to be in law enforcement and still fit God in there so He would be happy too! Brilliant! Then I hit another snag. I went to another youth conference in Hammond and heard Bro. Hyles preach again on seeking God's will for your life. Oh man, I had come up with a great plan and was just waiting for God to put His stamp of approval on it.*

Then a very big man named Jack Patterson came to our church. After the service, he came over to our house to spend the night. After everyone else had gone to bed, he called me out to our kitchen table and told me to sit down. This guy is about 6'7" and over 300 pounds. When he tells you to do something, you do it! He cut right to the point. "Jack," he said, "where are you going to go to college and what do you think God wants you to do with your life?" I told him my elaborate, impressive plan for reaching and ministering to every state police officer in America. He sat there patiently until I was finished. Then he cleared his throat, leaned across the table, looked me dead in the eyeballs, and said, "That is all real interesting, but I asked you, 'What does GOD want you to do with your life?'" I sat there stunned. He continued, "As you told me your plans, I heard an awful lot of 'I' and 'me' and 'my,' but I didn't hear very much 'God' and 'He' and 'His' in that whole deal." Again I sat in silence, cut to the heart. Here I had been building a great plan I wanted God to approve, instead of me yielding to whatever God's plans were for my life. I looked back across the table and said, "Bro. Patterson, you're right. That is my plan, not God's." That night with much encouragement from a modern-day Goliath of a man, I told God, "Not my will, but Thine be done." Oh, how glad I am that I made my college decision based on God's plan for my life and not mine.

Teenager, I beg you, seek God's will in the matter of your calling and if and where you should attend college. Not your will, your plan, your dream, or your desire, but may His will be done.

3. Choose the place that will best train you for that calling of God.

Let me first point out that no matter where you go to college, you will to a great extent become a product of that school. One of the main things that will transpire during your college years is a forming of what you are and who you are by the things you learn and experience at college. In light of this truth, it would do you well to examine carefully the overall product of the colleges you are considering. Ask yourself and others this question: "What school is producing the most successful graduates in my field of study or area of calling?" For instance, let's say that you feel God has called you to be a missionary. Don't you think it would make sense that you should become the best missionary you can be? Then make a list of as many great missionaries over the last 10-20 years as you know and find out where they went to college. Do you feel called to pastor a church? Then make a list of the best 100 churches in America and find out where their pastors were trained. Do you feel called to teach in a Christian school? Then ask and find out where some of the best Christian school teachers are and find out from where they graduated. You will to a great extent be only as successful as you are trained to be.

Now, let me stop and say that you will find graduates that supersede the average graduate of each school. You will also find underachievers from every school. Don't make your whole decision based on one super graduate or one dud! Overall, what colleges are right now producing successful missionaries or successful pastors or successful assistants or successful teachers and, even more importantly, successful Christians? If the list from the last five years is short or non-existent, maybe you should reconsider your choices.

It is also extremely important that you realize you will more than likely be selecting your mate from the college you attend. Therefore, it is vital that this school is properly preparing young people to be good husbands and wives. Girls, to the extent that your husband is successful, you will be successful. No one wants to be married to a flop. So if you believe God wants you to marry a preacher someday, you had better go to a school where they train successful pastors. If you feel God wants you to marry a missionary, it would be nice if you marry a missionary that knows what he is doing so you can stay on the field. Guys, if you want a good wife, go to a school where they teach the young ladies how to be good wives.

4. Go to an independent, fundamental, Baptist, separated, soulwinning, King James Version, old-fashioned, church-run, pastor-led school.

Now, I understand that it is not God's will for every young person to go off to college. But if God has directed you that way in your heart and through the godly counsel of your parents and pastor, this type of Bible college should be your choice. If this does not sound appealing to you, I apologize. This book was written to help godly young people find, do, and follow God's will. I understand that not all Christians are called into what we call "fulltime Christian service." However, every Christian in the world is called to be a fulltime Christian, and you will best be trained to be that kind of a Christian at the above-listed type of school. "But Bro. Bachman," you say, "I feel God has called me to be a doctor." If you have sought counsel with your pastor and together believe beyond a shadow of a doubt that is what God has called you to do, go to the above-listed kind of school. I know they don't offer medical training there, but if you become a successful doctor and do not learn how to be a successful Christian -- you lose. If you become a successful doctor but marry a girl that doesn't know how to be a good wife and end up divorced -- you lose. If you become a successful doctor but don't spend your weekends serving God faithfully in your local church -- you lose. If God has called you to be a doctor, train and prepare to be the best doctor possible. But before you start that training, you had better go some place where you can find the right kind of a mate, learn how to walk with God, get a good knowledge of the Bible, and find out how to teach a Sunday school class or run a bus route. The only way to be successful in anything is first to be successful in God's eyes. He tells us that the fear of the Lord is the beginning of knowledge and the beginning of wisdom. I promise you, they won't be teaching you much fear of the Lord at the state university so start with the basics and go somewhere that you can learn the beginning of knowledge and wisdom. If you make it through that step, then go take your medical training. But please, don't live in the state university dormitories. Do not do much of anything at that school or with those heathen besides go to class, take your tests, and get your degree. Stay actively involved in a fundamental, independent, separated, soulwinning, local Baptist church.

This point and this chapter are not meant to be exhaustive, doctrinally instructive dissertations on why or why not you should attend state universities or what is wrong with colleges that have no local Baptist church under whose ministry they are a part, but please seek godly counsel before you run off to some "Christian" college because it has nice facilities, it is near the beach, it is accredited, or it has a great sports program.

When you go to visit a college, make sure you attend a church service at the church that runs the college. For about four years of your life, the man behind the pulpit will be your pastor and you will be regularly hearing his preaching. Make sure the church has good standards, strong soulwinning, hot preaching, and balance. Make sure it uses the right Bible, has people moving at the invitation, is baptizing converts, is running buses, has godly music, and is growing. Don't choose a college or church where you would have to drop or lower your standards to fit in with those around you. Your college days should be days of spiritual growth. You can't follow teachers, leaders, or pastors that are not further down the road of righteousness than you are. Don't go to a college that teaches soulwinning and separation, but doesn't practice it. Make sure that soulwinning and separation are not just for the students but for the teachers and administrators as well. To a great extent, you will learn as much if not more about the ministry on the weekend in church as you do during the week in the classroom. Choose a church and a pastor that will cause you to grow closer to the Lord and give you the opportunity to serve God, win souls, and change lives. Make sure also that the leadership of the church is running the college and not the leadership of the college running the church! What you learn in the classroom on Monday you should be seeing in practice at church on Sunday. And what you hear preached from the church pulpit ought to be lived on the college campus. In summary, if the church isn't right, you are at the wrong college!

5. Find out what your strengths, interests, callings, and gifts are and head in that direction.

Now, I don't expect any seventeen or eighteen year old to know exactly what he is going to be doing for the rest of his life. If the truth is known, statistics show that most young people change college majors at least once and that a very small percentage ever end up with their major becoming their actual life's occupation. College is one of those times and places to find out what God has for you. By the same token, if God has already laid a burden and a calling on your life, pursue it!

Obviously, God's will is not just **one** of the goals, it is the **only** goal! Because God designed you with that will and purpose in mind, He has already placed within you some talents and interests that with the proper honing and molding will equip you to fulfill His will successfully. Discuss these things with your parents and your pastor to understand better what God is doing in your life and wants to do through your life.

I promise that whatever gifts, abilities, and talents God has given you, He will also provide opportunities to use those for Him. As Paul told Timothy in *I Timothy 4:14, "Neglect not the gift that is in thee"* and in *II Timothy 1:6, "Stir up the gift of God, which is in thee."* And he also told us in *Romans 11:29, "For the gifts and calling of God are without repentance."* Prepare yourself to use these for the Lord.

Chapter 4

Protecting Your Relationships

We have already discussed somewhat the need not to shun underclassmen your senior year and to do all you can to make as many memories as possible, but I want to put a little more detail into the importance of the relationships you need to protect. You are about to start a brand new part of your journey and meet a whole lot of great people. The people you meet and relationships you have in college will in some cases be friendships of a lifetime. By the same token, all relationships you have had up to this point are about to change. Let me help you with both.

First, let's talk about your current relationships and friendships. As I already mentioned, fight hard not to pull away from your peers as a senior. Also be very careful not to fall away from your parents, teachers, and pastors. These people have invested their time, sweat, tears, and life into you. I must warn you that when you come back from college, things will be different. At some point, though you still love your parents dearly, you will catch yourself calling college "home." This is entirely natural. College will be the place where you spend most of your time, where you make new friends, and where you live. But more will happen than you just calling college home, it actually will become home. You are starting a phase of your life where you are maturing, spreading your wings, and learning to fly all on your own. During this period of your life, be careful not to abandon your parents. It will be easier for you to leave than for them to let go. Call them on the phone and keep them updated on what is going on in your life. Write them letters thanking them for all they have invested in you. Though your relationship with them is about to hit a new phase, don't sell them out to spend time with some old buddies. On your first trip home for Thanksgiving or Christmas, spend your first couple days with Mom and Dad. Don't go running off and leave them in the dust. Protect your relationship with your parents.

The same is true with your siblings. Being the youngest child in our family, I know what it is like to have your older brother or sister come home from college. Even though they won't want to admit it, your siblings will have missed you and will want to spend some time with you. Believe it or not, they look up to you and will be glad to have you home. It wouldn't even hurt to send them a note from college every once in a while. You may be the biggest influence on where they go or don't go to college. Protect your relationship with your brothers and sisters.

Remember the youth group? When you go back, be friendly and tell them what a wonderful thing Bible college is. Your youth pastor has been preaching, working, and praying for many of those teens to go to Bible college when they graduate. If you are not careful, you can undo months of progress in the life of some highschooler in a matter of a few days if you come back with a negative spirit or a critical tongue. Be careful. By the same token, you are the best billboard your college could ever buy. Go back and live what you have been taught, talk about how exciting it is, and get very involved. Nothing is more discouraging than to see a young person come back from Bible college and sit like a bump on a log. Get on a bus route, even if you are only home for one weekend. Go soulwinning, sit up front at church, dress up, and dress right. Move at the invitation, be in Sunday school, and sing out during the congregational singing. Get involved in everything you can at church, whether you are home for one day or all summer. Many people are going to base their whole opinion about the Bible college you attend on your testimony when you come back. I would recommend that though you should be friendly to the teenagers, don't hang out with them. You have entered a new stage of your life. Don't go backwards. Don't try talking your youth pastor into letting you come to youth activities. Don't invite yourself or accept invitations to teenage functions or get-togethers. Spend time with adults or other college-age young people. Again, don't have an air of "I'm too good for you now," but rather just keep yourself busy with other things and older people. Protect your relationships with your former youth group and underclassmen friends.

Last in this category, make sure that your pastor, youth pastor, and teachers have the joy of seeing some fruit for their labor. Jot them an occasional note from college too, and tell them how glad you are for their investment and how thrilled you are to be in God's will. You have no idea what an encouragement this will be to these dear people in your life. There will be many days when they feel like they are beating their heads against a brick wall and making no progress. An occasional reminder that someone made it and is doing well may be exactly what they need to push forward one more day, preach one more sermon, counsel one more teenager, teach one more class, and not quit. When you come home for a visit, be a breath of fresh air to them and let your life be a reminder of the fact that their labor is not in vain in the Lord. Don't wander from what they have taught you, and keep on doing the things they have preached to you and the things in which they have instructed you. Protect your relationships with your pastor, youth director and teachers.

Beyond these old relationships you should work on protecting, you are about to build some new ones. The best relationships are built on the right foundation so be very careful with whom and how these new friendships are formed. Here are a few basic guidelines you should follow:

1. Be a friend to people older than you.

It will be hard for another new freshman to help you adjust to college life, find your way to class, or give you a word of advice from the voice of experience. Choose a friend who can help you make good decisions based on fact, not based on a guess no better than you could have made on your own. When my wife and I started dating in college, some of our dearest friends were about half a dozen senior saints at First Baptist Church in Hammond. We sat with them on Sunday nights and Wednesday nights. We talked to them before the services. We told them of our experiences of the week, and they brought us homemade cookies! They gave us words of wisdom and encouragement. To this day when we go back to Hammond to visit, we still see some of these dear saints of God and enjoy our fellowship with them. Now I am not saying that all your friends should be over sixty years old, but I am saying we learned a whole lot more about life, marriage, work, money, and living from these dear old saints than we ever would have from some twenty-year-old kid who was just as dumb as we were!

2. Be a friend to people more mature than you.

Now let me stop to point out that just because someone is older than you does not automatically make him a good choice for a friend. Unfortunately, maturity and age do not always go together. This is a time of your life when you should be maturing into adulthood. That will be hard to do if your best friends are still little kids in adult bodies. Probably the college student who is the class clown and is always playing practical jokes on people will not be your best choice for a new best buddy. This kind of a friendship will slow down your own maturing process and probably end you up in a lot of trouble. I am not saying you can hang out only with duds. I am just saying you should make sure your friends are having fun serving God instead of having fun cellophaning toilets, filling roommates' briefcases with shaving cream, and supergluing the professor's test file drawer shut. (For other great practical joke ideas, please call me at... just kidding!)

3. Be a friend to those who motivate you spiritually.

Don't take it on as your personal ministry to be friends with all those struggling spiritually hoping that you can help them. There is going to be a wrong crowd at every school, every college, every work place, and even every church. The more time you spend with this group, the worse off you will become. "Well," you say, "who is the wrong crowd?" I'm glad you asked! Anyone that encourages you to do wrong, think wrong, talk wrong, walk wrong, dress wrong, listen to the wrong music, go the wrong places, criticize authority and rules, or think less of someone is the wrong crowd. By the way, I would also avoid friendships that allow you to be comfortable with your level of spirituality. You need to develop friendships where time spent together encourages you both to think better, talk better, dress better, do better, win souls better, and serve the Lord more. I have a friend named Kenny Brooks. Though I don't see him as often as I used to, he and I are true friends. When we go soulwinning together, we motivate one another to win more. When we talk together, we challenge one another to do more. Almost every conversation that we have turns to what we have learned in our Bible reading. This keeps us both searching diligently for things to share with one another from our Bible reading. Our friendship causes us both to be better Christians because we challenge each other, motivate each other, and encourage each other. How about your friendships? Where do your conversations usually lead? How much better of a prayer life, walk with God, soulwinning fire, or a strengthening of convictions have you caused in the life of your friends?

4. Be a friend to those going the same direction as you.

If you are like most young people, you probably think that you MUST have a best friend. You also think that you somehow must find, win, and maintain that friendship. You will notice that each of these numbered subpoints have said, "**Be** a friend." I don't know that I ever set out to **get** a friend in college.

49

*Just do what you are supposed to do and you will look over one day and see others doing the same right beside you. These are the people with whom you will build the best and longest-lasting friendships. This is because your hearts are in the same place. Matthew tells us that where your treasure is, there will your heart be also. You might be saying, "I sure wish I could get a good spiritual friend." May I suggest that if you will just concentrate on **being** that kind of a friend instead of **looking for** that kind of a friend, God will send that kind of a friend your way. If those you are around are constantly hearing from you the answers to prayers you are having, the things you are learning from God's Word, the soulwinning experiences you are having, and the decisions for God you are making, those not wanting to discuss such things will soon find others to be around. If by your conversation, motivation, and way of life people can tell you are not going the same way as they are, they will either pass you by or turn around to walk with you. The Bible says, **"Can two walk together except they be agreed?"** You just keep your focus on being a friend to God and going in His direction, and those going the same way as you will be by your side.*

5. *Be a friend to the college faculty and staff.*

No, I am not talking about what is commonly known as "brownnosing." Now think about it, who do you think is best equipped to help you prepare for the ministry, for marriage, and for life? These college teachers were chosen for a reason. Listen to everything they say in class but, more importantly, watch them. I promise you that you can learn just as much if not more by observing them than through listening to them lecture. When I went to Hyles-Anderson College, I decided that I would learn one character trait from every teacher that I had. It would usually take only one or two classes before I had picked out one area in their life in which they were stronger than I was. From then on I would watch them closely every class, every time I would see them in the hallway, every church service, and every chapel service. I would look for examples of that one strength and try to improve myself to be more like them in that area. In one of my professors, Judson Mitchell, I saw the greatest heart of compassion I had ever seen. In Bill Grady, it was a brilliant mind who had mastered balancing intellect with common sense. In Carl Laurent, it was a man of true soulwinning fire and conviction. In Larry Smith, it was a man of prayer. In Ray Young, it was loyalty. In Dr. Jorgensen, it was work ethic. In Darrell Moore, it was family. In Pete Cowling, it was enthusiasm. In Jeff Owens, it was character. In Dr. Evans, it was humility. In Jack Schaap, it was preaching. In Dr. Hyles, it was all of the above and more. In some, it was humor. In some, it was personality. In some, it was a positive spirit. I also choose three men who I believe were a good balance of many of these things: Jeff Owens, Toby Weaver, and Jack Schaap. I watched the way they talked, *walked, sat, ate, shook hands, carried their Bibles, laughed, preached, sang, cried, scratched their heads, and blew their noses. Seriously! Though I never attempted to become their "friend," I studied them so carefully that I felt I knew them well. When I go back to Hyles-Anderson to visit or see these men around the country, I feel as though I am greeting some of my dearest friends. Have your pastor help you choose some staff members where you attend college to help counsel and guide you during your college years.*

I hope that you will build some great lasting friendships during your college days. Be careful to protect your previous relationships. Be careful to start new relationships on the right principles, and work hard at being the right kind of friend.

Chapter 5

Protecting Your Finances

*One of the most frequent things that keeps young people from going to Bible college or that knocks them out of Bible college is improper management of finances. Now many young people think it is the **lack** of finances, but that is usually not true. The average young person has thousands of dollars pass through his hands during his teen years. The problem lies in bad savings habits, wrong priorities, lack of work ethic, and lack of character. Again, this chapter is not meant to be an exhaustive study on money management. I do, however, hope to give you a few guidelines and principles that, if followed, will pay for all your teenage expenses and all of your college bills. In addition, this will provide some savings towards your future wedding, honeymoon, and beginning of married life without having to go into debt to do it.*

1. Start working right away.

I know that this piece of advice may be coming too late for some of you reading this chapter. No matter how old you are now, however, it is time to start working! When my sons were just a couple months old, I would wrap their hands around the bottle and hold my hands around their hands as I fed them. Slowly, I applied less pressure, and before long they could hold their bottles on their own. When they got old enough to sit up and play, I would hand them toys to put away. As they got older and started to crawl, I would have them bring me toys and help put them in the toy box. When they got big enough to walk, they threw away their own diapers after they got changed. Before Ryan was tall enough even to push a lawn mower, he was begging me to let him mow the lawn. Even though he wasn't big enough to take the big trash barrel to the curb, he was big enough to bring all the small trash cans from around the house to me to empty into the can. All this came from a heritage passed down from my father who had me busily working from the time I can remember. Helping raise and butcher rabbits, picking acres of green beans, collecting earthworms for a bait shop, picking and selling strawberries, mowing neighbors' lawns, pulling weeds, cleaning swimming pools, cleaning gutters, raking leaves, shoveling snow, cleaning horse barns, bailing hay, helping with church mailings, painting, and cleaning are just a few of the many jobs my father made sure were available to keep me busy. A couple years before I graduated, I started working construction in the summers. With every job I had, I never missed a church service, a special revival meeting, a youth activity, or a soulwinning session. It can be done!

"Great," you say, "what does this have to do with

money?" As long as you have a mind to work, you will never have a problem finding employment. There are plenty of people out there willing to pay someone to do something if that person will just show up, work hard, and not quit. Our biggest problem in the American economy is not unemployment, but rather unwilling workers.

Before your first year in college, you will have had close to twelve years to earn money. "What?" you ask. "What kind of money can I make as a five year old?" Not much, but more important is what you do with the money you do make. Start a savings account as soon as possible. There are many banks that provide "college bound" accounts that offer higher interest rates with no minimum balances and no annual fee or monthly service fees. You just have to put money in there and leave it until you go to college. Before you are ever even in the youth group, you should easily be able to have saved a few hundred dollars towards college. It is said that if a teenager has saved and invested $8,000 by the time he is sixteen years old, it will be worth over $1,000,000 by the time he turns sixty years old. Pretty good retirement plan, huh? Start working, start earning, and -- more importantly -- start saving.

Now let me be very clear. As I mentioned before, you will have the rest of your life to work and earn money. Be in a hurry to work but not in a hurry to get a job. There is plenty of work to be done for which people will pay you without you having to be tied down to a job as a teenager that will cause you to miss youth activities, church, ball games, soulwinning, bus routes, and memories. (Besides, many bad things often accompany a lot of teenage employment.) Start mowing lawns, babysitting, raking leaves, shoveling walks, cleaning gutters, pulling weeds, cleaning horse barns, walking dogs, and washing cars, and you will be amazed at how much money can be made as a teenager without sacrificing the joys and opportunities of adolescence. If you don't learn how to work, you will always have financial problems.

2. Start tithing right away.

Don't be pulled into the common misconception that tithing is for adults or for those that have a "real" job. Tithing is for everyone! If grandma sends you $5.00 in a birthday card, that is called "increase" and God expects fifty cents in the offering plate Sunday. If you get an allowance, you need to tithe. If you babysit, you need to tithe. If you mow the neighbor's lawn for ten bucks, you need to tithe. I would also encourage you as a teenager to get involved in offerings and missions giving. Even as a college student I was able to give to many special offerings and special projects because I had been taught at an early age that giving is a good investment. It's true -- you can never outgive the Lord. If you want to make sure you have your needs met, you had better not be stealing from the One who can meet them! Tithing is a habit that you need to get into for the rest of your life. It is never too early to start obeying God.

3. Start saving right away.

There will be no other period of your life when you will be able to save a bigger percentage of your earnings than as a teenager. You will be able to make a lot of money as a teen without an exorbitant amount of bills. You should be able to earn enough money to tithe, pay for your youth activities and teen camps, help with some of your regular expenses, and still put away at least 50% of your income towards college. I promise you that there will be no other time that you will be able to designate 50% to savings. Take advantage of this time in your life.

If you don't have the character not to spend the money, do one or more of the following. Open a savings account where they don't allow you to withdraw the money until you graduate. These accounts often offer a much higher interest rate too! If you blow money easily and your parents can be trusted, have them hold money for you towards upcoming expenses like camp or missions trips until they take place. Don't get an ATM card where you can easily withdraw money from your account. Don't get a credit card and don't take out a loan for your school bill, a car, or other things you may want. If you get paid in cash or check, go to the bank immediately and deposit everything but what you need to pay your tithes and that week's expenses.

4. Stop spending right away.

The average teenager spends at least $15 a week on pop and junk food. Hundreds of dollars are spent on music and clothes. One of the biggest financial black holes for teenagers is automobiles. If at all possible, DON'T get a car. Car payments, car insurance, car maintenance, fuel, tires, and brakes will quickly drain finances that could have easily paid for one or two semesters of Bible college. "What? No car?" you say. Yes, it can be done -- believe it or not. I never had my own car until I graduated from college. I worked between one and three jobs at a time and always had transportation. Most of the jobs I had as a teenager were close by my house. I either walked, rode my bike, carpooled, or had my parents take me. I promise that your parents would much rather taxi you around for a few years than have to pay your college bill because you spent all your money on a car. In college I also found ways to get to work. It was much cheaper for me to help pay for someone else's gas expenses than to have my own car. This also meant I couldn't easily run to the store to spend money or be out cruising, wasting gas and time. I'm not saying that it is wrong for you to have a car; I am just warning you that it is very expensive.

Be careful about eating out a lot. Even fast food is

very costly compared to food you could get at the grocery store. Once you get to college, you will be paying room and board. This usually includes your food in the dining hall. In most cases, you pay for those meals whether you eat them or not. To be paying for a meal at the college you are not eating while you are sitting in Burger King paying for a meal you are eating is not a really smart financial decision. Again, I understand that sometimes your schedule will not allow you to eat the meals provided, but when you can, eat the meals for which you already paid!

5. Start planning right away.

There are a lot of expenses that you will encounter in the next five to seven years of your life. You need to come up with a plan, or you will not make it financially. If you don't have a plan, you will either never have the money to start college or be financially withdrawn and lose your credits for the semester and have to pay for them again. It would be wise for you to try to have the first year's tuition paid for in full when you go to college or the first semester at the minimum. This will allow you to get settled into your freshman year without the pressure of possibly being withdrawn on week three because you gave every cent you had in the registration line and haven't been able to earn any more. You should try to get a job right away, but having your bill paid takes off the pressure and allows you time to find a *decent job instead of a bad job. By following this plan, each year you will be working to pay not for your current school bill but for your next year's bill. Continue your savings habits, and each year you can pay off your entire year's school bill on opening day. By staying a semester to a year ahead on your bill, you will be able your senior year to be earning money that can go towards a wedding, a honeymoon, a place to live, and a vehicle. There are plenty of pressures in college. Don't bury yourself needlessly under a financial burden.*

Here is another quick financial planning tip. If you are paying as a full-time student, you are usually paying the same amount whether you are taking twelve credits or eighteen credits. If you take only twelve credits each semester, you will not make it through in four years. If you will take as many of those eighteen credits as you can handle, you will save yourself having to pay for another entire semester down the road. This can be a substantial savings. If you can take even more than eighteen credits, you will have to pay above the regular tuition amount; but if you can do this each semester, you may be able to finish in three and a half years -- again saving a whole semester of tuition and room and board. You do need to make sure that you can handle the credit load before you try this. Saving money is not as important as you doing your best, getting good grades, and finishing the courses you start. Read the next chapter on scheduling before you try this.

Even when in college, you can do some things to earn a little extra money along the way. For instance, the summer before my first year of college, my dad had me go down for an hour a week and watch the barber cut hair. To be honest, I was not very thrilled sitting there watching him when I could have been somewhere else. A few weeks before I left for college, my dad very bravely had me cut his hair. I purchased an inexpensive set of hair clippers and headed off to college. I really didn't think that this little idea of my dad's was going to be very useful. Before I ever made it through the registration line, I had already given three haircuts. For the next four years I was giving haircuts regularly. The money I made from haircuts alone paid for all my textbooks, all my laundry, and a little extra spending money for dates and snacks. I also cut my own hair, saving myself between $600 and $800 over my college career.

I also walked anyplace I needed to go within a few miles of the college, saving me having to pay anyone gas money just to run me down to the bank. One summer I was working three jobs. I would get off my afternoon job around 9:00 PM and carpool back to the college. I would quickly change clothes and catch a ride with another guy that lived close to the steel company where I worked third shift. When I got off at 7:00 in the morning, I would walk back to the college from South Holland. Where there is a will there is a way, and it's often cheaper!

Another good moneymaker is typing papers. With almost everyone now having personal computers or laptops, it has become much easier to type one's own papers, but some people either don't have a computer, can't type well, or just don't have the time. College girls especially can make themselves available to type papers and charge a few dollars per page to do it. This helps other students save time and helps her make money.

What I am trying to say is that there is money to be made and you don't have to live under a huge financial pressure while in college. If you work hard, tithe faithfully, spend frugally, and save consistently, you can protect your finances.

Chapter 6

Protecting Your Schedule

Another common thing that knocks people out of college or prevents them from becoming productive in life is a lack of planning, organization, and schedule. It is vitally important that you develop an organizational plan and follow it. In this chapter we are going to discuss briefly a few different aspects of schedule.

1. Class Schedules

First, it is vitally important to develop an overall plan for your required credits. Once you have chosen a major, look to see what the required classes are for that particular course of study. Next, talk to some graduates or upper classmen who have taken or are taking the same major and have been good students getting decent grades. With their help, organize each class from hardest to easiest based on difficulty of teacher, tests, and outside work. Once you have these in this order, space them out over the eight semesters somewhat evenly. This will prevent you from having a lot of tough courses all in one or two semesters, from getting bad grades, from having incomplete assignments, or from facing discouragement. There may need to be some adjustment because of "prerequisite" courses or courses restricted to only upper classmen. For the most part though, I would recommend following this basic format. Space out the eight hardest courses over the eight semesters taking the least two hardest of the eight during your first and last semesters. This will not overload any one semester or year and will make your first and last years the easiest. Your freshman year you will be still getting acclimated to your new environment, roommates, personal schedule, job, and ministry. You want that first year to be a little easier until you get familiar with college life. Your senior year you will be focusing on marriage, a new potential position, and your last chance to make college memories. I would also recommend taking your list of classes and spreading out the eight easiest classes over the eight semesters. Many young people make a big mistake of saving all the hard classes for "later," and when "later" comes, it is too much to handle. Have a master plan and follow it. Seek counsel also from the college registrar or other staff who can help you even out your class load.

Next, as mentioned in the previous chapter, take as many credits of what is considered a "full load" or "full-time" as you can properly and adequately handle. You may be paying, as a full-time student, the same amount of money whether you take 12 or 18 credits (may vary in some colleges). If you take only 12 credits per semester for 8 semesters, that comes to only 96 credits, which will leave you short. You will then have to pay for another whole semester or more to finish up your required credits. Thus, it would make good sense to take as many of those 18 credits as possible since you are paying for them anyway. Again, you may want to take a little lighter load your first and last semesters or years.

If you are a good student and are not struggling with even the full 18 credits in a semester, you may want to talk to the college registrar about getting permission to increase your load to 20 or 22 credits. You will have to pay a little more for these extra credits, but if you can do that for a few semesters, you may be able to finish in three and a half years and save yourself an entire semester in tuition and room and board. This will more than compensate you for the small additional fee for the extra credits. Some colleges offer good summer school plans which again, for a small fee, may save you an entire semester down the road.

I am not encouraging you to rush through your college days or courses. I am encouraging you to be wise in setting your class schedules and save yourself spending unnecessary time or money if you are capable of doing it faster and cheaper. Let me be very clear. If you can get straight A's but rush through and pile on so many credits that you get B's, you have cheated yourself, your parents, and the Lord. You are expected to do your best in everything and to do it as unto the Lord. You need to find your load limit and do as much as you can while not sacrificing quality for quantity. Have the character to push yourself to your limit, as well as the character to back down if you start doing things half-heartedly just to get it done. I would much rather see a student who struggles with studies take six years to finish school but get every assignment done, get the best grades he can, learn something in every class, and graduate than to pile on the work, get grades lower than his capabilities, rush through, learn little, and either quit or graduate having cheated himself out of the kind of education that was available to him. Seek counsel, plan properly, and protect your class schedules.

2. Personal Schedules

You are about to enter a phase of your life when you will have more irons in the fire than at any other time in your life thus far. You will be trying to juggle work, classes, study, ministry, a walk with God, and dating. If you don't get a little organized and set up some type of a schedule, one or several of those things will go undone and you will not succeed. I am not going to attempt to lay out a detailed schedule that each student should follow, but rather again offer a few tips to help you make sure everything gets done.

First, start with some type of a **calendar**. Whether it be a Day-Timer, a Day Runner, a Franklin Planner, *or just some little pocket-sized calendar, get one! Often teachers in the first week of classes will either hand out or at least announce a schedule of test dates and due dates of assignments and outside reading. Write in your calendar each date announced or published for each assignment, test, or quiz for every class. Throughout the semester if the teacher announces anything upcoming, write it down on your calendar. Now at a glance you are able to see what is coming up in each class and plan accordingly. Every day look at your calendar and see what is due that day, that week, and that month. Don't worry about anything else until you see it is due within the next four weeks (unless it is something you are to be doing throughout the entire semester -- i.e., Old Testament Survey reading). This will help you plan, work, and study. It will also prevent the panic that comes from walking into class and seeing students feverishly cramming for a test about which they had also forgotten until they saw someone else studying. If this is as far as you incorporate these tips, you will be a world ahead of most college freshman!*

*Next, you need to have some type of a **checklist** or **"to do" list**. This is where you will write down what you need to be working on for that day, that week, and that month based on what you had written down on your calendar. This will also be the place where you can write down other duties or reminders about ministry, work, or personal items that you need to do. Again, each day look at this "to do" list and see what* needs to be done that day. Space out the reading, typing, or studying throughout the week to make sure you can reach and be prepared for each deadline for the week or month. When you accomplish that task or assignment, check it off and move on to something else still on the list.

Also, you need to set up some type of a **daily schedule** (see the samples in the back of the book). This may vary from day to day within the week but should be similar from week to week. Start by filling in your classes, chapel, work hours, ministry, etc., and then fill in the other things around the constants. I would recommend making sure that you schedule your daily time to read your Bible, pray, study, eat, shower, etc. Get as specific as possible without being restrictive. For instance, have a set time to study each day; but if you are all studied up, you can work on an upcoming assignment or extra outside reading. This is simply an outline for you to follow. As you go through your day, look for times where you have extra "unscheduled" time to fit in other things you need to get done. We all feel we are busy but have much wasted time within our day if we don't have and follow a schedule.

Last, you need to find ways to **maximize your time**. There are many times when we are doing something that requires little effort or thought that we could be doing something else at the same time. For example, in college many people will carpool to work and just sit there doing nothing. They may even have written *in their schedule "travel to work." While you are riding, you could be studying, reading, eating, or even sleeping. Maybe you could even be doing three things: riding to work, eating your lunch, and reading or studying. Now you are maximizing your time! On the way home, maybe it is too dark to read or study. Catch a quick 15-minute nap and when you get back to the dorm, spend 15 minutes studying. You just maximized your time! You have gotten the same amount of sleep you would have, but you also got 15 extra minutes of studying. In the shower, how much thought does it take to scrub your body and wash your hair? While showering, be quoting Bible memory you need to review or quoting a list of facts for an upcoming quiz. Spend that 10 minutes praying for a special need. Learn to maximize your time! Our time is just like our money. The problem is not usually that we don't have enough but that we don't properly use what we already have.*

All too often we look at a huge semester's worth of work and all the many things we have to do and think, "I don't have time to get it all done." You are right. You don't have time to get it all done today, so don't worry about it ALL today. Work only on accomplishing this week's work and preparing for this month. Break it down into bite-sized pieces. Prioritize what is important for today. Stick with your schedule and maximize your time, and you CAN do it! Getting into these habits and developing these organizational skills will be useful for the rest of your life. As you get older and your number of duties and responsibilities increase even more, you will be shocked at all you can accomplish if you will follow these steps.

Chapter 7

Protecting Your Health

Your college days can be some that put a strain on your health if you do not do some things purposely to prevent it. Your schedule is about to get much busier, your sleep will more than likely decrease, your eating habits and foods will change, your stress level will change because of new responsibilities and bills, and your environment is about to be different as well. All these things mean that you will need to plan and to work to keep your health a priority. Many college students have lost semesters' or even years' worth of credits due to poor health that often was a result of poor planning. Sick days mean missed classes, missed days of work, less money, more make-up work, and wasted time. It is also true that any health problems you already have will only become worse under these conditions if you don't become active in fighting against them.

I don't want you to become hysterical or paranoid; I just want you to be wise in taking care of yourself. I am not trying to turn you into a "health nut," but rather just asking you to become health conscious. In this chapter, I am going to list just a few practical things you need to consider to keep yourself in good health and minimize your sick days as well as the long-term effects that you could experience if you let yourself get run down.

1. Be careful about your sleeping habits.

Now, first let me start by saying that you can live on less than eight hours of sleep per night. You will not die if you don't get your beauty rest. It may even do you some good to not spend 56 hours of your week in bed. If you are used to going to bed early, getting up late, and averaging more than 7 hours of sleep a night, you may want to start revising your sleep habits now. You are going to feel like you are dying if you wait until your first week in college to start changing your sleep habits. I have worked third shift jobs before, and it takes a couple of months before your body really starts to get used to a new sleep schedule. If your parents have a set time that you need to go to bed, respect and honor that. By the same token, they probably will not be mad at you if you start getting up a little earlier in the morning. Start with 15 minutes earlier than usual, and do that for a couple weeks. Then take another 15 minutes off and so forth until you have weaned your body off of your usual 9 or 10 hours and down to something more reasonable for college life. I am not trying to play your doctor or parents; I am rather just trying to be the voice of reality and say that it is not reasonable that you need or will get that much sleep during your college years. By the same token, you do need to get some rest. Occasionally, going on little or no sleep is possible; but living on little or no sleep will ruin your immune system, cause you to not be able to think clearly, make you irritable, and may even kill you. I cannot begin to tell you the number of college students who have been killed or seriously injured in an accident when they fell asleep at the wheel due to a consistent lifestyle of very little sleep. I cannot give you a definite number of hours of sleep per night you need, as each individual is different. I can, however, make a few common sense suggestions.

For instance, sleep when you can. As a teenager, my brother and I were somewhat "night owls"; and even when I did go to bed early, I would lie there awake for sometimes and hour or more before I could finally fall asleep. College cured me of that problem. I learned to sleep anywhere, anytime. If you are coming back from work in a carpool, catch a 15 or 20 minute nap. It will really help you. When you get back to your dorm room, don't waste time. Get done what you have to do and go to bed. If you can do some of your preparation for the morning before you go to bed, it will allow you to do things more quickly in the morning. Be respectful of others in your room who are sleeping. You will want and need the same courtesy from them. Before you go to college, start learning to be able to sleep with a light on or small amounts of noise as dorm life will not always provide a completely dark and quiet atmosphere for you several hours at a time. You may have roommates that need to work late or get up early. You may even have roommates that talk in their sleep or snore. If you need to wear a sleep mask or ear plugs, do whatever it takes to assure you get good sleep. Often fatigue is not due to quantity of sleep as much it is to quality. And while we are on the subject, train yourself to get up to an alarm clock. If it takes three clocks spread across the room, do what is necessary to get you out of bed. However, it sure is more considerate to your colleagues not to have to listen to your alarm go off for 30 minutes straight before you hear it or every 10 minutes for an hour. It is time for you to grow up and learn to get up.

Regardless of what you think, you can't store up or make up sleep on a day off. You can't sleep for 24 hours straight and then go for three days without any sleep. The best plan is to get used to a certain schedule and stick to it. Getting up at the same time every day will train your body to the point that you will almost "naturally" wake up at that same time every morning. I didn't say "happily" -- I said "naturally!"

2. Be careful about your eating habits.

As we discussed in the chapter on finances, eat in the dining hall as much as possible. Maybe I should reword that. Eat in the dining hall as <u>often</u> as possible! Again, you have already paid for those meals, but beyond the fiscal sense, it will be much healthier for you too. I know it may not every day taste like your grandma's Thanksgiving dinner, but *those who are in charge of college dining halls do try to keep your overall health and diet in mind. I promise that it will be much better for your health than running through McDonald's every night on the way to and from work. Try to maintain a balanced diet as much as possible.*

Also avoid "living" in the snack shop. Almost every college campus in the country has a snack shop. Again, this should be a place to buy an occasional "snack," not the mainstay of your livelihood. Many college students have put on several pounds' worth of pizza and ice cream sundaes because they couldn't walk by the snack shop without at least stepping in to see who was in there that day.

Another pitfall is constantly "munching" in the dorms, or in your car, or at work. Learn to buy only gas and not always get a candy bar and a 64-ounce coke every time you stop for gas. If you have a check card, pay at the pump to avoid the temptation of that Krispy Kreme donut display case inside the station! If you spend a lot of time in your room studying, watch out for the consistent bag of potato chips or cases of pop at your side as your study partners. These foods will eventually catch up to you and cause you to become sluggish, unfocused, and unhealthy. Care packages from home are always a blessing, but don't consume the whole blessing cramming for one test!

Believe it or not, some people get so busy they forget

to eat. I must confess -- I am one of those strange people. If it weren't for my wife, I would probably have two-day stretches when I would just never stop even to think about being hungry. If my wife goes out of town, I have to force myself to remember to feed our sons. There have been times I am ready to put them in bed and my oldest son will say, "Dad, I am hungry." At first I think he is just stalling so he won't have to go to sleep. Then I realize I completely forgot to get us any supper. Not only does this make for tough explaining to my wife, but it also can be a bad health issue. If you are one of these strange sorts, make sure that you don't get so busy in college that you just don't eat much or very often. Food is your fuel; when you run out, you stall.

Be sensible. Eat the right food, in the right amounts, at the right times, and at the right price. Your health could depend on it.

3. Be careful about your exercise habits.

Oftentimes people mistake being busy for being active. Even though your college days may be hectic, you need to check to make sure you are staying physically active. If your job is not something that keeps you moving and sweating, you need to add some physical exercise to your routine. This will help keep your metabolism up and your overall energy level steady. Your metabolism is the average rate at which your body burns food. The higher your metabolism is, the more of your food you will burn and the less will go to be stored as fat. Find somewhere to walk briskly a few times a week or jump rope for 10 minutes a day. Get your heart rate up for about twenty minutes at least three to four times a week. You will be shocked at how much better you will feel, how much clearer you will think, and how much less you will get sick with just a little activity in your schedule. Other ideas are to join a sports team or an exercise group, or to take walks. Just do something active.

4. Be careful about your hygiene habits.

Again, there is no need for undue alarm, but you also need to be realistic. You probably used to have either your own bedroom or shared it with one or two siblings; now you have one, three, or more roommates. You used to share the bathroom with a few people in your house; now you may share it with dozens of people on the same dorm floor. You used to go to class with one or two dozen students; now you may have as many as 40 or more in your classroom. The bad news is that more people equals more germs. The good news is that the same precautions that will keep you healthy around five people will keep you healthy around five hundred. Just basic things like washing your hands regularly and not eating after others will help a lot. Beyond this, make sure you keep your room clean and help keep the restroom clean as well. Use a good antibacterial soap on your hands, an occasional Lysol-type air and surface cleaner in your dorm room, and keep your bedding and towels regularly washed. You can't live in a germ-free bubble, but you can be sensible. A little effort is better than a lost semester.

5. Be careful about your health habits.

Again, common sense is the key. If you are attending college in a place that has a climate different from what you are used to, watch and learn. I went to college at Hyles-Anderson just outside of Chicago, Illinois. It was always comical to watch the students from California with their spring jackets walking through two feet of snow on their bus routes. Learn to dress appropriately. Fashion is of little concern in 10-degree weather. Bundle up and keep yourself warm, dry, and healthy. You may want to take Vitamin C each day as it is a good immunity builder and helps fight off sickness. Take the extra couple minutes to dry your hair before you go outside. Zip up your coat, cover your head, and keep your feet dry. Okay, I am really starting to sound like your mother. The truth is that you are going to have to be your own mother. By that I mean you are going to have to remind yourself to do all those things your mother has harped and nagged you about for the first 18 years of your life. Believe it or not, as much as you hated hearing it, your mother was right. Use those common sense things to keep you in class, at work, out of the infirmary, and in good health.

This chapter may seem petty or ridiculous to you, I know, but you need to take heed to avoid being one of the countless college students losing classes, credits, money, jobs, and time because of unnecessary sickness. You need to be at your best in your classes, in your ministry, at your job, on your date, and in life. This will be hard to do from the infirmary. I also could give you many names of those who so destroyed their health in college that now years later they are still living with damaged immune systems and other lifetime chronic illnesses. Please be sensible and protect your health.

Chapter 8

Protecting Your Ministry

While in college, you are going to have the great opportunity to be very involved in saving souls and changing lives. This is called "the ministry." If for some reason this opportunity is not afforded you where you attend college, I would strongly advise that you are not at the right college! Nonetheless, you still are not excluded from this chapter. It is not only the privilege for every Christian to be involved in ministry, but also his duty. Whether you are in grade school, high school, college, or adulthood, it is for you. Whether you are a man or a lady, a preacher or a layman, a church employee or a construction worker, you are called to be a "minister." Therefore, you should be involved in seeing people saved, teaching them God's Word, and changing their lives. If you are not doing all of these, you are not doing God's will for your life. This may be in the form of doing one or more things like working on a bus route, teaching a Sunday school class, preaching in a nursing home, preaching in a jail, working in a children's ministry, ushering, singing in a choir, playing an instrument, or participating in any number of various opportunities.

Again, keeping a balance among these and your

other responsibilities is vitally important. More than likely, the problem is that you are not being involved enough rather than too much. Either extreme will be harmful and needs to be carefully maintained. Let me make a few recommendations.

1. Don't be pressured by any one person to join "his" ministry.

You need to realize that first of all we should all be on the same team working for the same objectives. If someone tries to talk you out of a certain ministry by telling you bad things about it or tells you that his ministry is the only one, that person has a problem. My first weekend in college, a very well-meaning, overzealous bus captain approached me and told me that it was God's will for me to be on his bus route. He further informed me that the bus ministry is the heartbeat of God and the only ministry I should consider if I really wanted to do something for God. Now, I was all in favor of the bus ministry and had been working on a bus route since I was eleven years old. However, this guy that didn't even know my name had no way of knowing God's will for my life. Furthermore, I believe the heartbeat of God is saving the lost whether they ride a bus, sit in a nursing home, drive a truck, serve in the armed forces, work in a bank, or sit in a jail cell. At 5:00 that Saturday morning he entered my dorm room, shook my bunk, and yelled at me to hurry and get out of bed or I would be late for his bus route prayer meeting. I rolled over, looked him in the eye, and very firmly told him that if he didn't get his hands off my bunk and get out of my room, his bus route would need to be praying for him! As of the writing of this chapter I have been a bus worker, bus captain, bus driver, or bus director for over twenty years. I love the bus ministry, but that doesn't mean God can't use me or you in other areas of ministry as well. Look closely at all the opportunities of ministry and seek counsel and pray to find out what God's will is for you!

2. Become the best soulwinner you can be.

Talk about the heartbeat of God -- this is it! No matter what ministry you may be involved in, you had better be able to show people how to be saved. If you can run a great bus program but don't lead your riders to Christ, you have missed the point. If you can plan a great youth activity but let the teenagers die and go to Hell, you have failed. If you go sing and encourage those in the nursing home but don't witness to them, what good have you accomplished? What does it profit a man if he gains the whole world but loses his own soul? You cannot baptize converts or teach them to observe all things until you first lead them to Christ. Learn to be a good soulwinner. Go to a college that is led by soulwinners, has classes taught by soulwinners, is under a church that is filled with soulwinners -- and learn to be a soulwinner. Don't get involved in a part of the ministry that ministers primarily to the saved *and think you are doing all God wants you to do. We need people to sing in choir, work in the nursery, and take up the offering; but we need choir members, nursery workers, and ushers that are keeping people out of Hell. Be involved in fulfilling the entire Great Commission. It all starts with soulwinning!*

3. Put your heart into it.

You ought to be putting as much energy and effort into your area of ministry as you do into the scholastic part of your education. You will learn just as much if not more on the weekends as you do in the classroom. All the head knowledge you gain Monday through Friday will be of little use unless you start putting it into practice Saturday and Sunday. We are talking about changing the lives of people for today and for eternity. This is a part of your college education that you will be using every week for the rest of your life. If you get a diploma but don't learn how to change a life, you have wasted four years and several thousand dollars. The Pharisees were very educated, but they weren't very smart. They were spending their lives following rules and teaching others but not affecting eternity at all. Give it all you have and don't just fill a few hours of required service. Ask God to use you to save souls, to love people, and to change lives. If you dread the weekend or find yourself bored, it is because you are not putting your heart into it!

4. Stay balanced and sensible.

While putting the excitement, energy, and heart into your ministry that you need to, please make sure you don't stop doing the other things you need to do. For instance, I know of college guys that got so involved paying for bus kids to go to Christian school that they got financially withdrawn from college and had to drop out and go home. How much help were they to those bus kids then? Stay balanced and pay your bills. I know of college students who were so involved in their ministry that they never had a date or found a mate. They left college still single. Those teenagers in their Bible club, kids on their bus route, or inmates at the jail are not going to cook their meals, clean their house, or raise their children. Maybe they should have stayed balanced, done a little dating, and found a wife. Others so filled their time with their ministries that they didn't do their assignments, study for their tests, or do their reading; and they failed their classes. Still others ended up oversleeping Monday mornings and over-absenced their classes while others made it to class but fell asleep in class and learned nothing. Maybe they should have stayed balanced and been able to show up and listen in class. This balancing act will be one they will need to perform the rest of their lives. One of the greatest pieces of advice my father ever gave me on this subject was this: "Son, I finally had to realize that I never have to choose between my family and my ministry because my family is part of the ministry. If I lose my kids to the devil or lose my marriage, I lose my ministry. When I spend time building my family, I am building my potential, my influence, and my work for God." That, my friend, is called balance! Start practicing it in college and learn to protect your ministry.

Chapter 9

Protecting Your Dating

One reason that your choice of a college is so important is because it will more than likely be the place you find your future husband or wife. Choose the wrong college and you will have trouble choosing the right mate. Dating is never mentioned in the Bible and yet the Bible has hundreds of verses pertaining to principles for choosing a mate. Dating as the world thinks of it and practices it is not God's idea at all. Dating is not a pastime, a game, an experiment, a status symbol, a freedom, or the chance for a free meal. Dating is the selection process for marriage. Just because you have reached a certain age does not automatically qualify you to begin dating. If you are not prepared to get married, you are not prepared to begin the selection of your future mate. Don't think you can jump out of the airplane door and worry about putting on your parachute on the way down. You had better get a handle on the purposes, principles, pitfalls, and procedures of dating before you go jumping into it. There are several great books out there on dating and much more information than I can condense in this chapter. There are also a lot of worldly philosophies and unbiblical suggestions out there. My highest recommendation for principles for choosing a mate is a book that has been around for a very long time with a 100% success rate by those who have followed it. You may find one in your local bookstore or borrow it from your pastor, or you may already own a copy. It is called...the Bible! I would highly recommend you read it and learn from those who have studied it closely. I am not trying to teach you all the principles of dating in this chapter, but rather mention a few words of wisdom in how your dating affects your college experience.

In light of this purpose, my greatest piece of advice is to PACE YOURSELF! For many of you, this may be your first opportunity to get involved in the dating scene. Don't be like a racehorse out of the gate and decide you will date everything of the opposite gender within the first two weeks of school! Here are a few pointers.

1. Don't get seriously involved with anyone your first year.

Over the years, I have watched many young people give their heart to someone within the first few months of their freshman year. More often than not, this situation ends up with one of the following results: they end up breaking up because they fell in love with the idea of falling in love more than with the person, they end up dropping out of school early so they can get married, they end up messing up morally, or -- at the best -- they end up living four very frustrating years very distracted from their schooling, their ministry, their other relationships and their walk with God. It will not take you long to fall in love and learn about the other person if you have spent the proper time preparing yourself. In my feeble attempt to analogize, let me give this illustration. I love to hunt. As many hunters can testify, you can sit in the woods motionless in the freezing cold for hours on end in anticipation of the monster buck. You may see many deer pass by, enjoy their beauty and grace, but never even sight them in. But when THE BUCK comes by and you have him in our cross hairs or have set the pin of the bow behind his shoulder, waiting is nigh unto impossible. Your heart starts beating fast, your body becomes tense, and no matter how cold it is you begin to feel hot and get tunnel vision, seeing nothing but the soft spot behind his shoulder blade. Welcome to dating! You can be in the woods, gun in hand, prepared, loaded, and in the hunt. You can patiently watch some pass by and never even have your finger twitch. But when THE ONE walks by and you get focused on his or her heart, holding your pose with that person in the cross hairs for four years before you pull the trigger is probably not going to happen. Enjoy the scenery, freshman, but don't put your scope on any one person this early when you still have a long time before you can pull the trigger. I believe the statement is not "Good things come to those who date," but "Good things come to those who wait." Don't get in a hurry on a decision that will last you a lifetime. If that certain person is God's will for your life, he or she will still be there next year. Don't think you have to bag your "trophy deer" now or he or she will get away. Hold your horses and show some patience and maturity.

2. When you start dating, keep the dates short and occasional.

It will not take you long to discuss with this person your past. You will be experiencing a large percentage of your present together, and so filling each other in on details or perspective won't take long. This leaves only one more thing to discuss -- your future. This topic of discussion can rapidly progress to marriage and all that it entails. You must understand that a girl has been planning her wedding since she was a flower girl at three years of age. When a guy pushes the "future" button, she has already spent almost twenty years preparing for that conversation. Spending hours on end talking or even having short discussions every day have great potential for leading to inappropriate conversations or a premature binding of the hearts before you even have the certainty of your future together. I would recommend unless the date is a planned group event that your time be limited to no more than two hours and no more than once a week to start. It is very easy for college students to start spending a lot of time together and often many times throughout the week or even several times in a day. Often they spend more time together than the waking hours of most married couples. *Even time spent together that you might not consider a real "date" will still keep moving the relationship forward. Don't think that you can sit together in chapel every day, eat lunch together, sit by each other in all the church services, talk for hours in the hallway, call each other ten times on the phone, and then have your one "real date" for the week and still be able to keep reins on your relationship. Once you get serious about a certain someone, your relationship will grow even when you're not together. When you are with that person, your heart will be going full speed ahead! If you don't control your time together, you won't do very well at controlling your emotions for each other.*

3. Keep your dates planned, organized, and active.

When you become idle in your planned conversation or activity, you become highly susceptible to wrong conversation and activity. Before any date, know what you will be doing and for how long. Plan topics of discussion and even back-up topics if some of those die out earlier than anticipated. If you fail to plan, you plan to fail.

4. Keep your dates properly chaperoned and your relationship accountable.

Properly chaperoned does not mean your five-year-old sibling, a bus kid, your blind and deaf grandfather, or your dog. It also, by the way, doesn't mean your "best friend," who would never tell on you, and his or her date. Choose someone whom you respect, who is spiritual, and who would either skin you themselves or call your parents on speed dial if you so much as try anything inappropriate. "What fun is that?" you ask. Well, try it your way and live with regret, a loss of testimony, a hindered walk with God, and parents with broken hearts. "What fun is that?" Take your parents, your pastor and his wife, your youth pastor and his wife, or some other godly couple that has not just a good evening but a great future in mind. As you progress through each stage of your relationship, you need to keep your parents, his or her parents, and your pastors or counselors informed and holding veto power. This starts with even the potential of a first date. The young man should get permission from his parents to ask the young lady out. If approved, he should then contact her parents for permission. He should also seek counsel about the young lady from his pastor, her pastor, or others that may have insight about her or the relationship. If you will do the proper investigation before the date, you will spare yourself a bad date or a potential break-up down the road. Beyond both sets of parents and your pastors, let me recommend a few others of whom you should inquire. First, talk to the person's employer. This will give you a reference concerning the person's work ethic and dependability. These are very important qualities and should be considered carefully. Next, check with the dean of men or dean of women and/or the person's dormitory supervisors. This should give you an overall report on the person's cleanliness, ability to get along with others, and discipline record. These too are vital aspects to know. Last, check with the person's ministry leader. Find out if he or she is involved, is faithful, is effective, is a good soulwinner, has a walk with God, and lives a godly life. If any one of these people gives you a "red flag" report, back away quickly so no one gets hurt. Often when a young person has followed this advice and has gotten two "okay" reports and one "red flag," he decides that two out of three is good enough and ends up regretting it either very soon or for the rest of his life. Seek good counsel and do your homework before you set out to have even one date.

If all goes well as the relationship progresses, keep your parents informed and stay accountable to them. It wouldn't hurt to give them the right and opportunity to read your letters, be in the room during a phone call, accompany you on your dates, or talk to your date privately. If they are unable or unwilling to do this, choose your pastor or another godly leader to help. If you have something to hide from them, you are doing wrong. I'm not saying they need to preapprove every word you speak or activity you do, but they should be able to do so without you having to change or hide anything. This accountability will keep you appropriate, moral, and properly paced. Now that you think I am way off the deep end, know that young people who have followed this openness have almost always stayed pure and without regret, and many who choose not to wish they could start over again. Just be glad you don't live in Old Testament days when your parents wouldn't just monitor your relationship, they would choose your mate and you wouldn't get to see him or her for the first time until your engagement, your marriage, or sometimes the morning after your wedding! Accountability to people who love you and have your best interest in mind may be inconvenient but will not be regretted.

5. Don't allow dating to get you out of balance.

I promise that dating is going to be more fun than taking sophomore English, more exciting than working third shift, and more exhilarating than preaching in the nursing home or swallowing a goldfish on your bus. Don't allow its glitter to draw you away from all the other things you should be doing. You are much better off throwing yourself into doing your best at everything and then one day looking beside you and seeing someone else doing the same. Every date is a potential mate. Date those going the same direction you are whose heart is in the same place as yours. If that person starts to weaken your walk with God, your ministry, your job performance, or your studies, they are not someone you want to marry. God gave Adam an helpmeet in Eve to complete him, to strengthen him, and to improve him. If this "potential mate" you are dating is not making you better in your walk with God, better in your ministry, better in your personal standards, and better in your life, don't doom yourself to a lifetime of failure. Be the right kind of Christian young person and you increase the caliber of person whom God can send you as a mate. Be a dud and God will reward you accordingly. If your dating is weakening you in any area, you are not right for each other. If your dating is not allowing you to fulfill all your responsibilities and opportunities, you are out of balance.

Chapter 10

Protecting Your Walk With God

No chapter in this book is more important than this one and no chapter will probably be less heeded than this one. If you follow every piece of advice in this book in every other chapter but lose your walk with God, you will not succeed. You may get a diploma, you may get good grades, you may even make good money, but you will not be a good Christian. No matter what profession you enter or from whom you receive a paycheck and whether or not you are considered in full-time Christian service, you are to be a full-time Christian. In order to do this, you must have a personal relationship with God. Going to church is not enough. Being a faithful soulwinner is not a substitute. Teaching a Sunday school class, working on a bus route, singing in the choir, or fulfilling some other church service is not sufficient. Going to a Bible college will not suffice. Even becoming a Christian school teacher, a youth director, or a pastor will not replace your walk with God. Furthermore, though any of the above listed things can be done in the flesh, not having your own personal time with the Lord will guarantee that you will not be a success or be pleasing to God. Your consistency, your effectiveness, and your joy in the Christian life are in direct proportion to your personal relationship with God. I think you would be shocked if you knew what a small percentage of Christians have a consistent and fruitful walk with God. How about you? Have you faithfully read your Bible and spent time in prayer every day this week or this month? Unfortunately, Bible college is one of the easier places to let this important part of your life start to slip. You will become a lot busier than you have ever been thus far. You also will be hearing a lot of preaching in chapel regularly. In addition, you will be attending classes every day where good Christian people will be teaching you and sharing biblical principles with you for sometimes four or five hours a day. You also will be actively involved in serving in a local church. Don't allow the devil to make you believe that any or all of these things will be sufficient and negate your need to spend time alone in God's Word and in prayer. Even with all the Bible knowledge and Christian service you may gain during your college years, if you are not careful, these years may be the ones in which you will backslide most. Put that in combination with these same years being ones in which you will make some of the most important decisions of your life, and it could certainly spell trouble. It will be very difficult for you to choose the mate of God's choice if you fail at your walk with Him. It will be very hard for you to find your place of service for the Lord if you are not faithfully spending time with Him. Let me give you a few very basic guidelines to follow to insure that you don't neglect the most important part of your Christian life during some of the most important years of your life.

1. Choose a place where you will meet with God.

No person will set an appointment with someone without establishing a place to meet. In my home, I have a particular place where I will read my Bible every morning and spend time with God. I also have three places where I have different prayer times. When we go on vacation somewhere, the first thing I do when I walk into the motel room is choose my place to meet with God in the morning. Choose a place at college where you will meet with God every morning. Let me recommend that lying down on your bed with your head on your pillow and the covers pulled up nice and tight will probably not be a real profitable situation. Choose some place where you can sit up, pay attention, have good lighting, and not easily fall asleep. During your college days, you may find that you get so tired that sitting anywhere for more than ten minutes may mean a certain nap. May I suggest that you try your praying and or reading while you walk. I found a little cluster of bushes on the back side of the lake at Hyles-Anderson while I was walking around the lake praying one day. I ducked inside and found a little hollowed out spot in the middle of those bushes. I worked at clearing the area enough so that I could pace back and forth in that small circle. That became one of my favorite places to go and pray. Some very sweet times of prayer and many important decisions were made in those bushes. It became my little Bethel. If you are ever going to have a consistent walk with God, you must first choose a place to meet with God.

2. Choose a time when you will meet with God.

It is also reasonable to acknowledge that it would be hard to have a meeting with someone if you didn't set a time. Have you ever been talking with someone you had not seen in a long time and said, "Hey, we ought to get together some time and have lunch or go do something." And they say, "Yeah, that would be great!" The conversation ends there and you never do get together. You both wanted to meet. You would have had a great time together if you would have met. Unfortunately, you never established a specific time. The same is true with God. We want to get together with Him. We would really be glad we spent time with Him if we ever did. Often, the problem is we never set a time. Again, this time may be different for each person based on personal schedules but let me make a few suggestions. First, I would recommend the morning. Even if you are not a "morning person," get up, take a shower, drink some juice, or whatever it takes to get alert and ready to meet with God. As we look through the Bible, we see many great examples of people who met with Him in the morning. The very first man, Adam, met with God early in the day. Abraham in Genesis 19 is found meeting with God early in the morning at the *place where he stood before the Lord. In Genesis 28 the Bible says that Jacob met with God early in the morning. Others like Moses, Joshua, Samuel, the priests, David, Daniel, and Jesus Himself are all listed as meeting with God in the morning. Now I understand that a true "walk" with God should be all throughout the day. But this time we are talking about is the first step of that walk. If you don't take a step with God, you certainly will not have a walk with Him. Again, if you were going to go walking with a friend, you would first set a place and a time to meet to begin that walk. David and Daniel established three times a day when they would talk with God. David also established a habit of having seven times throughout the day to praise the Lord. As you are to embark on your day, it would be a good idea to have talked with God and put on the armor of God before your day ever gets started. I am not opposed to you praying before you go to bed, but I would strongly suggest you also spend some time each morning with the Lord. I think there is also the principle of giving God your best and your firstfruits that you should consider. As your day goes on, you will get more busy and more tired. Give God the best of your day and the first priority, not whatever leftover time or energy you may have at the end. I don't want God to think I will work Him into my schedule if I get a chance or when I have all my things for the day completed. I would rather seek FIRST the kingdom of God. Choose a time or times that you will meet with God and don't be late to your appointments!*

3. Choose a plan for what you will do when you meet with God.

Now that you have chosen a place and a time, it would be nice if you knew what you were going to do when you get together. Many times young people go to camp where they have planned for them a scheduled time to meet with God. They just sit there thumbing through their Bibles and looking around and daydreaming, not having a clue what to do. Now there is no set plan written in stone for every person to follow, but if you don't plan anything, you will probably accomplish nothing. Here are a few suggestions you can try.

   a. Read Proverbs every month. Proverbs is full of wonderful guidelines and principles. These were written by the wisest man in all the world. Can you imagine if the President were willing to meet with you for five minutes each day? Or maybe some great athlete was willing to spend a few minutes every day privately helping you improve your game. Or maybe the richest business man was willing to meet with you every morning and give you advice on how to make millions of dollars. You have a greater opportunity than that! You can meet with and learn from some of the greatest Christians ever and then spend time with God Himself! Solomon gives some great advice to his son but is also willing to share the same advice with you. Read one chapter of his proverbs each day and you will complete the whole book each month. Pay attention and follow his *advice, and you could spare yourself many mistakes and heartaches and gain great wisdom for life.*

   b. Read through the book of Psalms. *You can do this twice in a year just by reading one chapter a day or every month by reading five chapters each day. David had a great walk with the Lord and knew how to praise the Lord better than anyone in the Bible. Reading these psalms will open your spirit, encourage your heart, and teach you how to trust the Lord more. We are commanded to use this special book to praise the Lord, be filled with the Spirit, and admonish and encourage one another.*

   c. Choose a certain subject you want to study, and read passages about that subject regularly. *You might want to know more about prophecy, and you could read Daniel and Revelation each week or each month. You might want to know more about the New Testament church and read the book of Acts each week or each month. Maybe you want to know more about the life of Christ and could read the Gospels each month or each quarter. Read the Books of the Law (Genesis - Deuteronomy) each quarter. Learn more about doctrine by reading Paul's epistles. This can be done in combination with other Bible reading you may choose but allows you to concentrate on studying certain subjects or aspects of the Bible.*

   d. Choose a certain chapter or passage you want to memorize and read it every day for at least

a month. *This is one of the easiest ways to memorize Scripture. Reading a passage at least once or twice a day for a month or two will ingrain it in your memory for life. There are many chapters that I memorized by this method as a teenager and college student that I still know today.*

*   e.* *Try reading through the Bible each year.* *By reading about four or five chapters a day, you can easily read the entire Bible. I would recommend getting a Bible reading schedule or chart so you can mark it off as you go. If you do not have one, there is one provided for you in the back of this book. If you are already reading Proverbs, Psalms, or other passages, you can skip those chapters when you get to them on your schedule. Some passages won't seem as interesting as others, but God wants us to read His entire Word and gain a good knowledge of it all. If you got a love letter from a girlfriend or boyfriend, you wouldn't skip over part of it would you? Even though you may have certain parts that mean more to you than others, I am sure you would read it in its entirety. Don't skip part of God's love letter to you!*

*   f.* *Determine to learn one new thing from the Bible every day.* *This does not even have to be some life-changing, spiritual truth. Maybe just try to find out what a "furlong" is or how much a "shekel" is worth. As you learn these new things, write them down in the margin of your Bible so that each time you read that passage again you will understand and*

picture what it means. If you learn one new thing a day from the Bible, that is 365 things a year. In ten years that is over 3,650 things you can learn and understand about the Bible. This is how you begin to "master" God's Word. Get a good dictionary or Bible dictionary and start today learning one more thing. Learning and understanding God's Word can be exciting.

g. Do word studies or subject studies as you go along. As you are reading your Bible and come across a certain word or subject, look up other places in the Bible that talk about that same word or idea. I remember once reading through the Gospels and continuing to see the word "immediately." I went to my concordance and found every time in the Gospels that when Jesus did something or said something, the result happened "immediately." That is a word study. I have looked up every time in the Bible it uses the words "marry," "marriage," "marriages," "married," "wife," "wives," "husband," "husbands," "espouse," "espoused," "divorce," "divorcement," etc. That is a subject study. These types of studies will not only make your Bible reading time more interesting, but will also allow you to start to know God's Word with understanding. The Bible tells us, **"Study to shew thyself approved unto God, a workman that needeth not to be ashamed, rightly dividing the word of truth."**

h. Ask the Holy Spirit to speak to your heart each day as you read. One of the jobs of the Holy

Spirit is to guide us into all truth. Before you start your Bible reading, ask the Holy Spirit if He will please point out something you need from your Bible reading today. Certainly, all of us have many areas in which we need to fix something, change something, delete something, add something, or improve something in our lives. Certainly the Holy Spirit knows what those things are and wants us to change them, and certainly, He can use the Bible like the mirror it is to show us our condition. The problem is that we often don't read God's Word, we don't pay attention to it, we don't listen to what the Holy Spirit is trying to say, or we don't want to change what He points out to us. If we will honestly and sincerely ask the Holy Spirit to speak to us and change us, He will! Just think about how much we could grow if we made one improvement a day. I challenge you just to try it!

*i. **Develop a prayer list of things and people to pray for daily.** There are many things and people for whom you should be praying daily. Make a list of these and try to spend time praying for them every morning. There is no set list that you must have or follow, but I will give you a few ideas to get you going. Every day you should pray for forgiveness of any sins that the Holy Spirit brings to your mind. The best time to confess a sin is immediately when you realize what you have done, but at least every 24-hour period try to make sure your slate is clean before God. You should daily pray for God's power, wisdom, and love. I would also recommend that you* daily ask God for His help concerning your specific weaknesses and your various responsibilities. Beyond these very basic things is a whole list of people that need someone praying for them as well. These may include your government leaders, your family members and other relatives, your church leaders, your employer, your future mate, missionaries and other men and women of God, and other friends or acquaintances. As you can see, just praying for these people specifically can take quite a bit of time. If your list of people continues to grow, maybe you can split it up and pray through it once a week. One caution -- don't allow your prayer list to become a memorized, vain repetition. Think about what you are saying and see it as more than a list of names. Each of those names has special burdens and needs. Occasionally, change the order to keep you from rattling it off like a Baptist rosary! A good rule of thumb is to pray as earnestly for others as you would want someone to pray for you and your needs.

j. Keep a list of specific requests that you will pray for until they are answered. This will be a great encouragement as you see God answering your prayers. When people mention a request that they have, add it to your list and leave it there until you can check it off and write a date that the Lord answered it. You will be amazed at the multitude of prayers God is willing and waiting to answer for those that are willing to pray. The reason we seldom have answers to prayer is because we seldom pray.

God said, "Ye have not because ye ask not."

k.   Have certain times that you just go off somewhere alone with God without a daily list or a request list and just talk with the Lord.   These seasons of prayer may be related to a major need or decision you have or may be just to recharge your spiritual battery.   Not much will put you back on topside like a long period of time sitting at the feet of Jesus.   Even if when you start it seems a little awkward, stay there anyway and listen.   Prayer should not just be a one-way conversation.   No, you shouldn't be hearing any voices, but God sure will bring things to your mind if you will be quiet long enough to hear what He has to say.

4.   Start where you are and build from there.   If you currently have no real plan for a daily walk with God and devotion time, don't think you will start meeting with God for an hour or two each day.   Follow these steps choosing a place, a time, and a plan and incorporate a few things at a time.   Maybe you can try reading your Proverb for the day and praying for five people.   After you seem to be consistent at spending ten or fifteen minutes a day, increase your reading and prayer time.   Don't get discouraged and quit just because you missed a day or only made it eight minutes.   That's better than where you were when you started.   Just keep building your time little by little.

5. Remember that a morning devotional time is only the first step of your walk with God. Often people think that because they met with God in the morning, that is sufficient until tomorrow morning. Don't leave God in your prayer closet and say, "See you tomorrow." Take Him with you all through the day. Establish different times throughout the day you will plan to talk with Him. Maybe as you drive to work, take a shower, eat your lunch, or exercise you could talk with Him more. And then at unplanned times throughout the day, talk to Him. A "walk with God" is best defined as "getting God involved in my life." That means before you take a test, go soulwinning, make a decision, answer the phone, have a date, start your work, or listen to a message, ask God for His help. And beyond that, just talk with the Lord as you go through your day about what is going on and what you are doing right then. Don't feel like God is not interested in the small details of your life or is too busy for what you might think to be only "small talk." Remember that He is with us 24 hours a day. How much of that time do you ignore Him? How would you feel if you spent all day with someone you loved dearly and that person spoke with you and acknowledged your presence for only about 30 minutes that morning and then never spoke to you again. I bet you would feel a little put out and overlooked, wouldn't you? I wonder how many times God feels awfully overlooked by us. Let's not only develop a consistent devotional life, but let us also build a real "walk with God" and start getting God involved in our lives all throughout the day!

Chapter 11

Protecting Your Attitude

It is imperative that you work hard at protecting your attitude during this important phase of your life. Your life is changing drastically. The pressures will be building, your responsibilities growing, and your schedule becoming more hectic. You will be attending a new church, getting new teachers, working a new job, and even having to deal with roommates. All these things can easily cause you to drop your guard and get a bad spirit if you are not careful. There are many problems that you can have with your attitude, but we are going to look at three main types of bad spirits from which you must diligently keep yourself.

Negative Attitudes

Let me start out by saying that no matter what college you attend, it will not be like you imagined. It will not be like summer camp or like a nine-month-long youth conference. It also will most definitely not be like home. The cafeteria food will be different from Mama's homemade cooking. Your dorm room will not be like your own bedroom. Your classes will not be like they were in high school. Your responsibilities will not be what they were when you were a teenager. And, if I might add, your roommates will not be like your siblings or your old best friends. In spite of all these changes, don't assume that means it has to be bad. Accept these facts and move on. Your college days can be some of your most exciting, memorable, and profitable if you don't let them be spoiled by a negative spirit. Countless good young people have left good colleges and never finished -- all because they let a bad spirit take root in their heart. Let me give you a few pointers to keep you from developing this dangerous attitude.

1. Stay away from negative people.

There are going to be gripers, critics, and complainers anywhere and everywhere you go. Don't allow someone else's negativity to ruin your attitude about your college, your ministry, your job, your roommates, or your church. A bad spirit is like a fast-spreading cancer that is contracted by listening to someone running his mouth about what he doesn't like or with what he doesn't agree. Get away from that person. It could cost you getting your college education, finding your future mate, or doing God's will. Find people that are positive, upbeat, and excited and make them your companions.

2. Look for good in everyone.

Believe it or not, since all of us are sinners, it is not too difficult to find bad in people. Force yourself to start looking for something good in each person. Once you have found that character trait, every time you see him, silently repeat that trait to yourself and pray and thank God for that individual. Before long, everywhere you go you will find yourself saying, "My, I am surrounded by so many good people." It will be hard for you to become critical, discouraged, or negative if you are constantly thinking about how good people are. I think it was best said by Paul who encouraged those at Philippi to think on things that were true, honest, just, pure, lovely, and of good report. Every Monday morning I have in my schedule a time where I write what I call "appreciation letters." Sometimes I write one, sometimes I will write several. This morning I wrote seven. This forces me to be looking all week long for good in people for which I can in turn compliment, thank, and encourage them. My, how it will change your outlook if you will stop focusing on the one or two things you don't like about each person and start looking for all the good things God has placed in those around you.

3. Spend time praying daily, thanking God for His blessings.

God has given us so many wonderful blessings every

day of our lives, but again we seem to focus on the few things we don't have instead of all the marvelous things we do have. One of my favorite verses is **Psalm 68:19** which says, **"Blessed be the Lord, who daily loadeth us with benefits, even the God of our salvation. Selah."** Not a day goes by but what God loads our wagons with blessings. We are usually too ungrateful, too apathetic, too impatient, and too selfish even to notice. The last word of that verse, "Selah," means to stop and think. Do that each day. Stop and think about how good God has been to you. The air you breathe, the health you have, your family, your nation, your freedom, your Bible, and your God are all gifts of grace! How could we ever be negative about life? David told us not to forget that He is not only the Lord, but also the God of our salvation. Now there is something worth being excited about having. Get your eyes off of what you don't have and start thinking about God's daily load of blessing He sends your way. If for some reason you can't think of how many good things you do have, spend some time thanking God for all the bad things you don't have. You could have cancer or poverty, you could be blind or deaf, you could be an orphan or homeless, you could live in a third-world country, or you could not be living at all. God is so good and we are so ungrateful.

4. Don't discuss negative things with anyone but God.

Now if you have a true problem, you need to tell someone. If you are sick or in pain, tell the doctor. If you know of wrong being done, tell an authority. If you need help, get it. But if you just have a gripe or something that is difficult, tell it to Jesus alone! Your mama and your daddy don't need you calling home every week telling them how bad you have it. First of all, you don't need to be dwelling on it or sharing it. Secondly, they don't need to hear it. Make it a point not only to look for positive things, but also to share them. If you're tired and your classes are hard, tell God. If your job is difficult and your tests even worse, tell God. If you don't like your roommates' bad habits or annoying tendencies, tell God. However, after you have just spent 15-30 minutes thanking God for how good He is to you, you probably won't even feel like telling Him about these picky little things.

5. Spend much time in God's Word.

The Bible is a great attitude adjuster. It tells of people who were treated much worse than you. It tells of people who had great faith in God to handle their problems. And it even tells of God's grace when things aren't going your way. The Bible says, "Great peace have they which love thy law: and nothing shall offend them." If you are developing a negative attitude, close your mouth and open God's Word. Keep reading it until God fixes your heart.

Apathetic Attitudes

The next bad spirit from which you need to guard yourself is one of apathy. This is the common "Who cares?" or "Whatever!" attitude of many young people today. This will most likely not happen during your first few weeks of college but after you get adjusted, get settled, get acclimated and get backslidden. Be very cautious not to allow yourself to get an "I don't care" spirit about anything. Watch your attitude concerning your classes, your roommates, your job, your ministry, your grades, the rules, your demerits, your finances, and your walk with God. When you stop caring, you stop trying. When you stop trying, you stop growing. When you stop growing, you start dying.

One great danger with these bad spirits is that you may be the last one to see what is happening to you. Choose someone who has a close walk with the Lord and ask him to keep an eye on you. Make sure it is someone who loves you enough to tell you if you are going astray. My first week in college I went to the Dean of Men, whom I had come to know very well, and asked him to watch me closely. I said, "Bro. Weaver, if you see me starting to drift, to get a bad attitude, to do wrong, or to hang around the wrong people, call me in your office and rip my face off." Make your attitude accountable to someone to keep you from self-destruction.

Pharisaical Attitudes

Another common attitude problem among college students is that of a pharisaical spirit. Somehow when an eighteen-year-old marches across a platform and gets a little piece of paper, he thinks he now knows everything and has arrived in society. I hate to burst your bubble, but what it really means is that you are capable of walking across a platform and carrying a piece of paper at the same time! Not to minimize your wonderful achievement of graduating from high school, but you have a lot to learn! Be careful to guard yourself from becoming a self-proclaimed know-it-all.

1. Don't be a Pharisee with your peers.

Don't forget it was just a few months ago you were one of those naive juniors. Don't make them feel like now that you are a senior or even a graduate you have the corner on knowledge and wisdom. I have seen all too often juniors and sophomores start despising their previously good friend who has now "arrived" and is too good to be around them anymore. And when you arrive at college, Mr. Know-It-All, your upperclassmen roommates will not be overly impressed with your great counsel and advice either. Better to be quiet and let them wonder if you are a fool than to open your mouth and remove all doubt!

2. Don't be a Pharisee with your professors.

It is a wise thing in college to ask questions about things you don't understand. It is not so wise to make comments about things you think you do understand. If the administration needs your expertise and insightful input, I am sure they will contact you by your sophomore year and offer you a full-time position. Until such a time, ask only related, sensible, and necessary questions. If you think you know better than the teacher on a certain point or issue, set up a private appointment with him and express your views then, not during class. If called upon in class, remember you were called on for an answer, not to entertain the class with your stupidity or to impress the class with your self-proclaimed wisdom.

3. Don't be a Pharisee with your parents.

I promise that as little as you think your parents know or as much advice as you think you could offer, that is all about to change. With each year that passes after your high school graduation, you will comprehend more and more of your parents' true knowledge and wisdom. Your parents are proud of you for finishing high school and moving on to higher education and maturity. Don't spoil it by thinking that now that you are an "adult" you can start telling your parents a thing or two. The command to honor your parents does not have a statute of limitations that runs out when you turn eighteen or even twenty-one.

4. Don't be a Pharisee with your pastor.

What a shame when a young person goes off to college and comes home for a visit and thinks that he or she needs to correct his home church pastor. Just because you took a church education class, attended some Bible classes, or were involved in a ministry, this does not give you the qualifications nor the right to criticize or correct your man of God. God is very clear in His Word that He will correct His servants when they need it and that He will punish those who take it upon themselves to try to lift up their hand or their tongue against His men. Just having a big day on your bus route or getting an "A-" in Homiletics does not make you the authority or the source of all wisdom. Your pastor probably has more power with God in his big toe than you have in your whole body. One thing is for sure -- he has a heap more experience, so you had better sit down, shut up, and pay attention. The things you learn at college may be of benefit if incorporated in your home church at your pastor's request. But if he doesn't ask for your counsel, there is a good chance you don't need to give it. Don't start sitting in a service back home and counting all the things that are "wrong." The one thing we know is wrong is your pharisaical attitude!

Chapter 12

Protecting Your Testimony

Solomon tells us that a good name is rather to be chosen than great riches. This word of wisdom comes from someone who had great riches and had the opportunity for a good name. He was the son of the great King David. He was the king of God's chosen people Israel. He was a king with God's blessing and wisdom. He had quite the chance to have a really good legacy and testimony, but he foolishly traded it for selfish and temporal pleasures. At the end of his years, in the book of Ecclesiastes, he looks back over his life and tells how empty and useless it all had been. He became famous for being the richest king ever and the wisest king ever, but he concludes that the only truly important thing is to fear God and keep His commandments. The only problem is that at this point it was too late for him to go back and take that path. He had only one chance to have a good name, and he blew it. You too, my friend, have but one opportunity to have a good testimony in this era of your life. Don't blow it. If you will succeed at this goal, it will be because you purpose in your heart, plan in your head and perform in your life the things that will keep your testimony blameless and blessed.

1. It is easier to work hard than to undo the testimony of laziness.

There are many young people that have gone through my youth departments and graduated that I would never hire as an employee in any fashion. They were good teenagers. Some were great soulwinners. Many were good bus workers. But they were lazy bums. No matter what area of profession you may enter, your employer wants to know first of all if you are willing to WORK. We are raising a lazy, wimpy, welfare-dependent generation of young people who don't know what it means to work. If they aren't guaranteed it is going to be fun, if it is going to take too long, or if they aren't going to get paid millions of dollars, they don't want to do it. Laziness is a snowball that will only grow bigger the longer you let it go and will eventually ruin you and many around you. Whether it be in the classroom, the factory, the bus route, the ball field, your house, or God's house, have a testimony of being a worker. You will never lack for opportunity if you know how to work. You also will never lack for promotion in this society of slothfulness. Be a worker. When people look at you, may one of the first things that comes to their minds be "Now there is a hard worker." What a fabulous testimony that would be! But for those who exhibit laziness, what a fast track to failure they are on.

2. It is easier to be mature than to erase the testimony of foolishness.

For the rest of your life your college roommates will remember you for what you did and what you were in the dormitory, not for what you may become. Your college days should be fun and filled with exciting memories, but don't taint them with immaturity and foolishness. No matter what level of success you may achieve, your colleagues will remember you as a freshman idiot if you don't work hard to protect your testimony in the dormitory. There are men today that are doing good works and serving God faithfully. But when I see them or hear their names, I am flooded with memories of the problems they caused on the dorm floor during their college days. It may be unfair, but it is reality. Don't make your name synonymous with the prince of pranks, the demerit king, or the class clown. Have fun, make memories, and enjoy your college days; but remember to act your age -- not your IQ!

3. It is easier to live purely than to overcome the testimony of promiscuity.

Someday you are going to marry and have children. For the rest of your life you will live with the testimony of purity or promiscuity and have to answer to them for it. You will never regret looking at your children when they ask if you stayed pure and telling them, "Yes, I did and you can too." But you will have a lot of shame and explaining to do if you expect them to do what you did not. You are also today building the foundation of your future mate's trust. Someday you will want to give that person the *security that you know how to exercise control and keep your hands off that which does not belong to you. Your future ministry may even ride on your ability to keep yourself pure. Even if you think your behavior is completely hidden and secret, God knows, you know, those with whom you have been inappropriate know, and God says that one day it will become known before all. How many politicians have their entire careers ruined because a skeleton they thought would never be revealed becomes the headlines in national papers and lead stories on the evening news. God puts it this way: **"And be sure your sin will find you out."** Don't have people remember you in college as the hall flirt, the loose girl, the playboy, or the dating machine. You will attract what you are, not what you want. Don't dress, act, talk, or behave in such a way that gives anybody the idea that you want anything but to please the Lord and to have God give you a spiritual, godly, and pure mate. If you dress to attract the flesh, you will attract fleshly people. If your talk is crude and shady, that is the kind of person you will get. If you are a major flirt, you will attract someone who is easily drawn away to lust. Be careful how you behave. God may give you what you are and not what you want. Therefore, if you want to marry a pure, trustworthy, faithful mate someday, you had better make sure that's what you are. You only have one chance to build a testimony of purity.*

Chapter 13

Protecting Your Momentum

Momentum is that part of the law of thermodynamics that says things that are in motion tend to remain in motion until slowed or stopped by an outside force. Simply stated, it sure is easier to keep something moving than it is to get it moving again once it has stopped. This is true with your education too. There are several things that can break your momentum and, in so doing, make it very difficult to get moving again. Let's look at a few.

1. Avoid a delay before you start college.

One of the many purposes of this book is to help you prepare so that when you graduate from high school, you can go right to college the next fall. You need to go while you still have momentum. Go while your math skills, parts of speech, and historical facts are still fresh on your mind. Go while you are still used to getting up for school every day and sitting in class taking notes. Go while you still are sharp on your studying skills. Just as it is with a muscle in your body, if you don't use it, you will lose it. There is no better time to head off to college than while you still have your momentum from high school. It would be really easy to stay out of school for a while and get used to a lighter schedule and different life. The longer you stay out of the "school mode" however, the harder it will be to get back into it and get the ball rolling again.

2. Avoid a break during college.

The best way to get through college is straight through! Even if you have to slow down a little and take an extra semester or extra year, try to avoid sitting out a semester or two. Most who do, don't go back. The reasons for sitting out a semester can usually be avoided by following the chapters in this book on finances and health. Though very few times it may be entirely unavoidable, if you must drop out a semester because of an accident or surgery, or some other drastic measure, get back in as soon as possible.

3. Avoid a wedding during college.

Let me make it plain that I am not trying to play God in your life or make a blanket demand for every person. I am just making a suggestion based on much observation of what seems to work and what usually doesn't. My reasons for this point are multiple. If both of you still have schooling left when you get married, you need to be aware of some potential problems. First, getting married and starting a life together can be costly, and having to pay for two college tuitions in addition to your other new bills will be difficult. Second, in order to make it financially you will need to go to school and then go to work, which leaves little time to see each other. This is a poor foundation upon which to build your marriage. In Deuteronomy 24, God told men getting married not to go to war or do any business for a year so that he could spend this first important year of their married life cheering up his new wife. (Pretty sad that it would take 365 days of encouragement for her to get over getting married!) Nonetheless, the principle is that the first few months together are vital and need your full attention. If the man is done with school and can go to work while his wife is in school, they still have their evenings together. This still will take proper financial planning but is workable. Third, along with marriage often come children. This will be an even bigger burden if you still have college classes to attend and pay for on top of a new mouth to feed. Fourth, many good couples get so accustomed to married life that they have trouble ever getting back into college. You, your parents, your teachers, your pastor, your children, and your future ministry deserve you finishing what you started. Finish this stage of your life before you jump into the next one. You need to give your best to your college days and to your married days, which is hard to do when you are trying to juggle them both. Fifth, having gotten married myself, having been involved in numerous weddings, and having seen countless other weddings,

I can testify that a wedding is not only very expensive but also is extremely time consuming. This is especially true on the part of the young lady. The groom-to-be will fill his last few months before the wedding day saying, "Yes dear," and "Sounds fine to me," and "That will be nice." On the other hand, the bride-to-be will fill each and every waking moment planning and re-planning each and every detail of the entire event. Even in her sleep she will be playing the ceremony over and over in her mind. With this being the case, little time and little thought will be left for studying for an English exam or doing a lot of outside reading. At best, she will be distracted and find herself doodling on her notes additions to the guest list or decoration ideas. I have witnessed firsthand girls making pencil drawings of bridesmaids' dresses during a college Bible class. It is rare for a young lady about to be married to have either the organizational skills or the mental discipline to stay focused on doing her best in her college classes while worrying about last-minute details of a wedding.

4. Avoid a delay after you finish college.

If you properly followed the advice you have received, you should be able to complete your schooling, have no outstanding bills, get married, and then be ready to jump into your next phase of service for God. Don't allow yourself to get too attached to your job, your home, or your new schedule. The whole purpose of going to Bible college was to prepare to serve God in some capacity. If this is to be full time, seek a full-time position and in the meantime be busy serving the Lord. If this is to be on the mission field, get busy on deputation and stay busy during deputation. A pastor and church want to see that you are already busy winning the lost and getting people in church here in America if you want their support to go across the seas to win the lost. If you went to Bible college primarily to get a spiritual foundation and find a good mate, get moving in the next step of your career training. Get into a good church and spend your weekends serving on a bus route, in a Sunday school class, or in other avenues of service. Don't get out of Bible college and just sit. God leads people who are moving. Don't "wait" on God and do nothing in the meantime. The longer you sit, the more comfortable you will become, the faster you'll rust, and the less likely you will be to do anything. You have made a good start by finishing Bible college. Don't waste months or years of service for the Lord once you have finished. Get out there and keep the ball rolling!

Plan carefully and work hard to avoid things that may slow down your momentum. I have seen many adults who carry much regret for not ever finishing high school or college. The same is true with many who are out of church. It usually boils down to a couple of problems they hit along the way that knocked them out for a while; and the longer they *were out, the harder it got to go back -- so they never did. Don't be one of this number. Most of the time they could have avoided the problem to begin with had they properly planned and prepared. But even in cases when it was out of their control, they still didn't push to hurry, to get back, and to keep the ball rolling. Once it comes to a dead stop, it is awfully hard to get it going once again. Protect your momentum.*

	SUN.	MON.	TUE.	WED.	THU.	FRI.	SAT.
6:00							
6:30							
7:00							
7:30							
8:00							
8:30							
9:00							
9:30							
10:00							
10:30							
11:00							
11:30							
NOON							
12:30							
1:00							
1:30							
2:00							
2:30							
3:00							
3:30							
4:00							
4:30							
5:00							
5:30							
6:00							
6:30							
7:00							
7:30							
8:00							
8:30							
9:00							
9:30							
10:00							